THE LITTLE BOOK OF
GOLF

Written by Patrick Morgan and Steve Newell

THE LITTLE BOOK OF
GOLF

This edition first published in the UK in 2006
By Green Umbrella

© Green Umbrella Publishing 2007

www.greenumbrella.co.uk

Publishers Jules Gammond and Vanessa Gardner

Printed and bound in China

ISBN 10: 1-905828-06-3
ISBN 13: 978-1-905828-06-7

Contents

Chapter 1

Origins
of Golf

WHERE IT BEGAN, NO ONE KNOWS. The origin is lost in the mists of time.

It might have been on a road in Normandy, or in a Roman alley. It might have been in dunes above the North Sea or on a hill overlooking Peking. It might have been in a Flemish field or a London courtyard, or on a frozen Dutch canal.

No one can say where or when golf was born, but one thing is certain: no other recreation has so transfixed its practitioners.

Hardly a country remains untouched by the golf epidemic. Its lure is hard to define, impossible to exaggerate. It's an obsession that can begin at any age and last a lifetime.

Golf's appeal stems from one of man's primal urges: to strike an object with a stick. Envisage homo erectus swatting stones or bones with a tree limb. So golf is older than civilisation itself.

Depending on whom we believe, the first golf shots were struck between 2,000 and 600 years ago. The Roman Empire's soldiers played paganica, hitting a feather-stuffed ball with curved sticks. But evidence suggests this was a team sport, and the ball was moving.

Scrolls from the Ming Dynasty (mid-to-late 1300s) depict suigan – "a game in which you hit a ball with a stick while

caught on in England, where it became the rage of the ruling class under the name 'pall mall' after the famous London street. Charles I was an avid player.

By the 18th century, this game had played out, except in southern France, where Basques would hit over hill and dale to targets such as barns.

In Belgium, chole was played, using iron clubs and an egg-shaped wooden ball. Two teams bid on the number of shots needed to hit a distant target. The low-bidding team took three strokes; their opponents had one stroke to send the ball into trouble. The offence took three more strokes, followed by one for the defence, and so on until the bid was hit or missed.

walking". Silk traders might have exported this game to Europe.

A 14th century stained-glass window in Gloucester Cathedral shows a figure wielding a stick with a golf-like backswing. But this might have been a game called cambuca.

Across the Channel, the French had a game called jeu de mail: a blend of billiards, croquet and miniature golf played with mallets and wooden balls. It

Whether these games of the Renaissance era bore any resemblance to golf is of little consequence, because by that time golf was well entrenched along Scotland's east coast.

ABOVE The ancient game of pall mall being played on the court

were pursued through churchyards and town centres and ultimately, the colfers were banished to the countryside. In winter, they shot towards poles on frozen lakes and rivers.

Colf was popular in Holland for at least 400 years. By the early 1700s, however, it had vanished, in all probability to Scotland. Note the connection between 'colf' and 'golf'; the implements and balls used were similar; and there is geographic evidence.

By 1650, golf was well rooted in a dozen towns on Scotland's east coast, a short sail from Holland. Scots exported wooden clubs to the Dutch, who returned the compliment with rudimentary colf balls. And paintings show Scots playing a stick-and-ball game on ice.

It was the Scots who gave golf its unique character; who combined distance off the tee with deftness around the green; who ingrained the notion of players advancing independently towards a hole.

The first written evidence of golf is a parliamentary decree banning it, for reasons of national security. In 1457, James II of Scotland declared "that futeball and golfe be utterly cryit doune

The best argument for a forefather of the Scottish game comes from the Dutch, who in the 13th century played a game with more than a passing similarity to golf. Its name? Colf.

In 1296 the Dutch had a colf course, stretching 4,500 yards for just four holes – or doors, rather – to a kitchen, a windmill, a castle, and a courthouse. Balls

and nocht usit". It seems the Scots, at war with England, had been neglecting archery practice in favour of golf.

When James IV married the daughter of England's Henry IV, the conflict with the English ended – and so did the conflict with golfers. James IV became the first of a long line of golfing royals, and legend has it that Mary Queen of Scots teed it up the day after her husband, Lord Darnley, was murdered in 1567.

In 1604, the King of England appointed a royal clubmaker, and soon after, a seven-hole course was laid out near London, on the Black Heath. Royal Blackheath still sits there today.

Despite royal approval, golf was open to anyone with a couple of clubs and a

BELOW A couple of golfers teeing-off whilst their caddies wait behind, 1862

ball. It was an informal activity, with no rules, few guidelines and no formal competitions.

Golfers learned to hit the ball on a low trajectory, keeping it under the sea breezes: feet far apart, bodies aimed to the right of the target, ball positioned well back in the stance and knees deeply bent. The club was whipped around the body horizontally and the ball flew a few feet above the ground. It would then run on after hitting the hard turf of the links.

As the game spread, methods developed, word of great play travelled and a

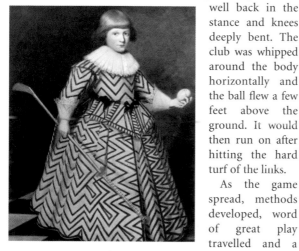

ABOVE Seventeenth century golf enthusiast with an early golf club and the large ball stuffed with feathers

desire arose to find the best golfer in the land. In 1744, golfers from the Links at Leith persuaded the city of Edinburgh to provide a silver club as the prize for an annual competition. The event was open to "Noblemen or Gentlemen or other Golfers, from any part of Great Britain or Ireland" and the winner would be called 'The Captain of the Golf'.

Ten local men played and the prize went to John Rattray with a score of 60 for two trips around the five-hole course – holes ranged from 414 to 495 yards. The event is recognised as golf's first organised competition, and the Leith golfers are credited with forming the first bona fide club, the Honourable Company of Edinburgh Golfers.

But that day something even more important happened: golf was played according to a set of rules.

They were brief – just 13 in all – and charitable, with no penalties for violations. The first rule stated: "You must tee your ball within a club-length of the hole." Imagine how craggy those early putting greens must have been.

Indeed, golf's first fields bore little resemblance to today's manicured meadows. The Scottish courses were set on linksland: barren, undulating terrain that separated beaches from arable ground. The sandy subsoil drained well but supported only long grasses and thick brush, making it of little value except to rabbits and sheep.

These herbivores served as golf's first greenkeepers – and played a role in course design by burrowing into the turf as protection against the elements. As the wind enlarged the burrows, bunkers took shape.

Those original courses had no tees, fairways or greens, just a hole in the ground every few hundred yards, but one might be as shallow as a rabbit scrape, the next so deep that retrieving the ball was a major achievement.

There was no set number of holes, either, with courses running according to the lay of the land. While the Links at Leith had five holes, nearby North Berwick sported seven. There was a 12-holer at Prestwick, and Montrose

weighed in with a whopping 25. In time, a standard would be set, and the authority for that decree would come from the bastion of golf administration, the little town of St Andrews on Scotland's east coast.

For golfers, St Andrews means one thing: the grandest of all links, the Old Course. Written evidence of golf at

BELOW Golfers attending the Open Golf Championship, standing outside St Andrews clubhouse, 1860

St Andrews dates from 1552, but most historians agree the game was played there in one form or another for at least 300 years before that.

St Andrews' golfers did not organise themselves into a club until 1754. On May 14, "twenty-two Noblemen and Gentlemen being admirers of the ancient and healthful exercise of the Golf" formed The Society of St Andrews Golfers and adopted the 13 rules set down by the Edinburgh golfers.

The first step towards St Andrews becoming the world's golf capital came in 1764, when the St Andreans made a revision to their playground. At that time, the Old Course consisted of 12 holes. Golfers played 11 holes out to the far end, turned and threaded their way home, playing 10 of the holes backwards to the same cups before finishing at a solitary hole near the start. Thus, a round consisted of 22 holes.

But in 1764, the Society decided to convert the first four holes into two. Since this change shortened the same

four holes to two on the road in, the round was reduced from 22 holes to 18, which would become the world standard.

Over the following years, the Society attracted the best and brightest golfers, framed new rules and positioned itself as the last word on all matters golf. When, in 1834, King William IV became the Society's patron and declared it the Royal & Ancient Golf Club, the pre-eminence of St Andrews was assured.

In 1834, however, there wasn't much golf to oversee. Only 17 clubs existed: 14 of them in Scotland, two in England and one in India. Throughout the world, fewer than a thousand people could call themselves golfers. And more than a few were women.

In 1811, Musselburgh fishwives participated in the first known women's tournament. The first women's club, St Andrews Ladies' Golf Club, was formed in 1867 and the Ladies' Golf Union followed in 1893, with the first official Ladies' Championship not far behind. The first three championships were won by Lady Margaret Scott, who was known for a long backswing, tremendous distance and scores in the 80s. After her third championship, Lady Margaret retired undefeated.

Doing less well, however, was the game itself. In the early 1800s, golf was shrinking. What a century earlier had been a recreation of the masses had eroded into a diversion for the wealthy and privileged.

Why? Above all, because of the ball.

BELOW Golfer Isette Pearson, wearing ladies golfing clothing of the day. Circa 1890

Chapter 2

Development of the Game

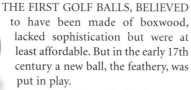

THE FIRST GOLF BALLS, BELIEVED to have been made of boxwood, lacked sophistication but were at least affordable. But in the early 17th century a new ball, the feathery, was put in play.

Consisting of a leather cover stuffed with goose or chicken breast feathers, it was about 1.6in in diameter but weighed only three-quarters of an ounce, about half that of a modern ball. The feathery provided resilience and distance: the strongest players could hit it over 200 yards.

A strip of bull or horse hide was soaked in alum water, then cut into two

circles and a strip for the middle. These were sewn together, soaked again and turned inside out. Into a small hole the ballmaker stuffed the feathers, boiled to make them malleable, with a 'brogue': a blunt-edged iron spike topped with a wooden crosspiece on which he leaned. When he had crammed in about a top hat-full of feathers, he sewed up the hole.

As the ball dried, the feathers expanded while the cover contracted, producing a hard sphere. The feathery was then hammered as round as possible and painted for protection against the elements.

ABOVE Two early featheries, circa 1850

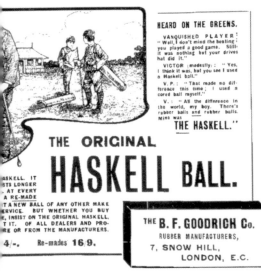

affordability would attract more people to golf. In the mid-19th century, that ball arrived in the form of gutta percha, the coagulated milk of a Malayan gum tree.

The substance was exported in sheets, which the ballmaker cut into strips, softened in hot water, and rounded by hand. The ball was then dropped in cold water to harden. If a 'gutty' became bruised or cracked, it could be resoftened and made whole again.

The first gutties were rounder than feather balls but, with no markings on their surface, they were tough to get airborne and tended to duck or dive in flight.

Willie Dunn, a Musselburgh professional, noticed his caddies were hitting gutties with more authority than he could muster from a feathery. The reason? Nicks and scuffs: once it had a few cuts, the gutty

Even the best craftsmen could produce no more than four balls a day, and featheries were 12 times more costly than wooden balls. What's more, one off-centre slash with an iron could knock the stuffing out of it, and players invariably required three or four balls per round.

What was needed was an inexpensive, weatherproof and more rounded ball; one whose performance, durability and

ABOVE Gutta Percha balls, circa 1890

TOP LEFT The Haskell ball transformed the game at the beginning of the 20th century

BELOW The modern golf ball such as the Titleist Pro V1 makes the game too easy (apparently!)

BELOW Golfers
Captain Hay Wemyss
(right), 'Old' Tom Morris
(left) and Allan
Robertson with his
clubs under his arm
(centre), at St Andrews
in Scotland, 1854

flew like a champion. So entered the hand-hammered gutty, with pre-chiselled aerodynamic markings.

Craftsmen began cranking out a hundred gutties a day, and tradesmen, artisans and peasants once again thronged the links. By 1890, the smattering of golf clubs in Great Britain had grown to 387 and golf had reached every outpost of the British Empire.

But the arrival of the gutty was met with opposition by one faction: the feathery makers. Chief among them was Allan Robertson of St Andrews.

Allan was the finest golfer of his time, is credited with being the game's first professional and was probably its first course architect

and green superintendent.

But the gutty threatened Robertson's livelihood. He made his employees promise never to use the ball, which led to a rift between him and his chief apprentice, Tom Morris, who agreed to shun the gutty but was caught out. He claimed he'd run out of featheries and was forced to borrow a ball, but Robertson was unconvinced. Morris opened his own gutty shop, first in St Andrews and later in Prestwick.

In time, Robertson gave in to the gutty, and he was also among the first to realise that the new ball required new clubs.

Golf had been played with essentially the same assortment of mallets for more than two centuries. The woods had shafts of hazelwood or ash with heads of apple or thornwood. The two pieces of wood were spliced together, glued and bound with tarred twine. The grips were of soft sheepskin.

The play club was a long-nosed

ABOVE Workers manufacturing golf balls, 1932

weapon with little loft in its tiny, high hitting area. Its shaft was 45in long but it met the clubhead at an angle of 120 degrees, forcing golfers to stand well away from the ball and contributing to the flat, around-the-body swing.

Lofted woods called spoons, because their faces were curved like the bowl of a spoon, were used for approach play, from the long spoon for distance shots to the baffing spoon for raising the ball from poor lies and over hazards. A golfer might carry as many as three putters, also made of wood: in addition to the traditional putter there was the driving putter for hitting low tee shots into the wind and the approach putter for bumping the ball in to the green. All were lofted.

Iron clubs were for dire circumstances, as suggested by their names: bunker iron, rut iron and track iron. Their heads had concave faces and snubbed-off toes.

As the ball changed, so did the clubs. The hard gutty yielded little at impact and wood clubs tended to crack on contact. So clubs appeared with shafts of a softer wood – hickory – and with less torsion: the clubhead lagged less far behind the hands during the downswing, which would lead eventually to a more up-and-down swing.

The clubheads also changed, to softer beechwood that absorbed the hit better, and became shorter and thicker to pack more punch. The ultimate effect of all of this was to lessen the strain on the spliced area just above the clubhead.

Iron clubs became the preferred implements for approach shots, and several Scottish blacksmiths took up clubmaking full-time, under the title 'cleekmaker'. The cleek –

equivalent to the modern 2- or 3-iron – was followed by the more lofted mid-iron, mashie and niblick.

Allan Robertson embraced the new irons as a craftsman and a player, and was probably the first to master the run-up shot with a cleek. At St Andrews in 1858, he ran his approach onto the 18th green then rolled in for a total of 79, making him the

BELOW Opening of the golf season at St Andrews, Scotland, 1876

first to break 80 on the Old Course.

A year later, Robertson fell sick with hepatitis and died aged 44. His death left a void in professional golf, and there was an urge to fill it. Tom Morris and Musselburgh's Willie Park were leading Scotland's players and rail travel had brought them within easy reach of courses.

In 1860, the Prestwick Club announced a championship for professionals, with a red Moroccan leather belt embroidered with silver medallions as the prize. Only eight men entered the first event, and the winner was Willie Park with an unimpressive 174 for 36 holes. The scores were so high that a number of amateurs felt they might do better, so the next year the competition was opened to all. And the Open Championship has remained so ever since.

When Tom Morris won the Championship for the last time, in 1868 at the age of 46, he became, and remains, the oldest Open Champion. One year later, the title was won by a lad of 17 years – still the youngest Champion. His name was also Tom Morris. This father-son duo would forever be known as Old and Young Tom.

Young Tom defended his title successfully in 1869 and took permanent possession of the belt with a third straight win in 1870.

There was a gap in Open play in 1871 for lack of a prize. Then, in 1872, St Andrews, Musselburgh and Prestwick presented a silver claret jug, and the three sites began a club-to-club rotation principle that continues today. 'Tommy' picked up where he'd left off, winning the title at Prestwick for a fourth time. He might have won it many more times had he not died aged 24.

In September 1875, as the Morris father-son team were closing out a match at North Berwick, Old Tom received a telegram, and told his son they had to leave immediately: his wife and newborn had died in childbirth. The young man played golf only twice more before passing away. The clinical cause of death was likely pneumonia but, in the lore of golf, Young Tom Morris died of a broken heart.

Old Tom outlived his son by 33 years, returning to the Royal & Ancient Golf Club as its first resident professional. With his long grey beard, tweed cap and

pipe, Tom Morris was a familiar figure to all who passed by his shop near the 18th green.

ABOVE 'Young' Tom Morris wearing the British Open belt which he won four times

Chapter 3

Spreading the Gospel of Golf

GOLF TOOK ITS TIME TO REACH the masses, but when it did, it spread like wildfire. The period from the mid-19th century to the beginning of the 1900s witnessed an explosion in participation.

Around 1860 there were 30 golf clubs in Scotland and three in England. By 1900 there were more than 2,000 clubs across the whole of Britain. Two main forces drove the boom.

First, the gutty, about a quarter of the price of the feathery, brought the game within reach of a wider audience. And enough gutties could be made to meet increased demand for balls.

Expansion of the railways was the other influence. More people started to take holidays, and seaside resorts built golf courses to attract visitors.

The Open Championship went from strength to strength. From 1872, a steadily increasing number of entrants competed for the Claret Jug and, with Old Tom Morris past his best, it was left to a new guard to take over. Jamie Anderson, a St Andrews man, seized the opportunity, winning the championship three times in a row from 1877–79, and Bob Ferguson followed with a hat-trick of victories from 1880–82.

The performances of two great amateurs lit up the Open in the final decade of the 19th century. John Ball

America it had barely taken off. Old Tom Morris played a role in changing that.

Scottish linen merchant Robert Lockhart visited his shop at St Andrews in 1887. Lockhart had emigrated to the US, but his job frequently took him to Scotland. He decided to introduce the

LEFT Golf at St Andrews, 1905

BELOW Harold Hilton in action

became the first golfer from outside Scotland to win, in 1890, and in his footsteps followed Harold Hilton, like Ball from the Royal Liverpool Golf Club.

Hilton's first Open victory at Muirfield in 1892, the first 72-hole championship, was sealed with a total of 305 – which was not bettered for more than a decade – and he won again in 1897. And in 1911 he became the only Brit ever to win the US Amateur Championship.

Golf in Britain was soaring, yet in

BELOW
Jamie Anderson inspecting golf clubs at St Andrews in Scotland

game to friends in America and, in Morris' shop, purchased six clubs and two dozen gutties. Six months later, Lockhart's friend and fellow Scot John Reid assembled with five other gentlemen in a cow pasture in New York, to give golf a try.

All six became instant converts and founded a club they named the St Andrew's Golf Club, in honour of the home of golf. So November 14, 1888 became the official beginning of golf in the United States.

Within five years of the founding of St Andrew's, dozens of clubs had opened, aided by a stream of emigrant Scottish professionals. Scots had also spread the gospel of golf to all corners of the British Empire.

India was the first to receive the game, with the opening of the Royal Calcutta Golf Club. Australia followed with Royal Melbourne in 1891 and New Zealand, Mauritius, Canada, Hong Kong and South Africa were next. In continental Europe, too, golf was getting a grip: France and Belgium were among the first to build courses.

While many Scottish professionals were in a hurry to get to the US, Charles Blair Macdonald went the other way. The son of a wealthy Chicagoan, Macdonald sailed to St Andrews in 1872 at the age of 16 to study. His grandfather bought him a set of clubs at Old Tom Morris' shop, and soon he was spending every spare moment on the Old Course, learning from the great players.

Two years later, Macdonald returned to the States with a passion for the game. But, since the US was devoid of courses, he made do for 15 years playing on trips to Britain. Once America got the golf bug, however, Macdonald was ready. In 1894, a group of amateurs assembled at the Newport Golf Club in Rhode Island to determine a national champion, and CB was the man to beat.

But when he lost by a stroke to William Lawrence, Macdonald protested that a stone wall, which had cost him two strokes, was not a legitimate hazard, and that a proper championship should be decided in a head-to-head format.

He got his wish when St Andrew's held a second amateur championship,

this one at matchplay. Macdonald defeated Lawrence in the semi-finals, but, after halving the final match, lost to Lawrence Stoddard in a play-off. This time he argued the result was invalid because one club may not presume to run a national championship.

Lawrence Curtis, of The Country Club in Brookline, Massachusetts, and St Andrew's founder Henry Tallmadge agreed to invite representatives of clubs to form a body to conduct national

ABOVE The 6th Hole at Muirfield Golf Club

BELOW Golfers playing on the links at Biarritz, France, circa 1910

championships and further the interests of the game. And so, in December 1894, the United States Golf Association was founded.

The association's first president was businessman Theodore Havemeyer, with Macdonald settling for second vice-president. A year later, however,

BELOW Golfers playing on the links at Biarritz, France, circa 1910

Macdonald got what he really wanted – a victory in the USGA's first Amateur Championship, held at Newport. Macdonald blazed to a 12&11 victory over Charles Sands, a young tennis buff who had played golf for just three months.

The next day, 21-year-old Englishman Horace Rawlins bettered nine fellow professionals and one amateur to become the first United States Open Champion.

Macdonald's breakthrough was also his swansong – he never won another championship – but he did have a lasting influence on the game, as America's first great golf course architect. In 1895 his bold design at the Chicago Golf Club – a seaside-type course set a thousand miles from the sea – became America's first 18-hole course. But Macdonald's masterpiece was a layout on the eastern end of Long Island, a course which he modestly named The National Golf Links of America.

Macdonald poured several years and many thousands of his dollars into it, and when the National opened in 1911, it set a new standard for American golf architecture. In the clubhouse

is a life-sized bronze statue of CB Macdonald. Legend claims he commissioned it himself and billed members for it.

CB wasn't afraid to feed his ego in his course design. He routed the Chicago

ABOVE A group of golfers under an Old Douglas Fir on the 15th Green of Banff Springs golf course, circa 1939

Past golfing champions and competitors at the Open Gold Championships at Muirfield, 1929

graceful pivot, dazzling footwork and overlapping grip that Harry Vardon had made famous. However, while the great man's technique was much admired, the golf ball that bore his name, the Vardon Flyer, had just about flown its last. Another new ball made its way to the tee. And it changed everything.

Coburn Haskell was an entrepreneur and keen golfer who dreamed of longer drives. One day, visiting the offices of the BF Goodrich rubber company, Haskell noticed a basket full of elastic thread. He had a brainstorm – he could wind those thin strands of rubber around an inner core and make a golf ball that would surely be more resilient and lively than a gutty. Haskell got a ball wadded up and persuaded BF Goodrich to fashion a gutta percha cover for it.

The result was America's first major golf invention: the Haskell ball. It flew

Golf Club's holes in a clockwise circle to favour the left-to-right drift of his shots. Spray the ball to the right and your worst penalty was light rough; spray it left and you were in a cornfield. Since this inequity was too severe, a three-word phrase made its debut in the rule book of 1899: out of bounds.

Americans wanted to play with the

fully 20 yards farther than the gutty and hit the ground running. Initially, increased bounce and roll made the Haskell difficult to control, but for anyone in need of distance, it made golf a different game.

After short-hitting Walter Travis used it to win the 1901 US Amateur, the ball known as "Bounding Billy" was embraced by America and soon the Goodrich Company was mass-producing them on an automatic winding machine.

But it had its critics, among them the British Sandy Herd who, on the eve of the 1902 Open championship, denounced the ball as unfit. But during a practice round, Herd got a lesson in playing the Haskell from amateur John Ball, and changed his mind. The 1902 Open went to Herd by one stroke over Vardon, still flogging the ill-fated Flyer.

BELOW A view of the 3rd hole at the Oakmont Course

BELOW The 9th hole of the Pine Valley Golf Course

The Haskell changed everything, beginning with the implements that struck the new ball. The softer, more springy Haskell required woods with a harder hit, and persimmon became the tree of choice, with inserts of various materials. Iron heads were enlarged and scored with grooves to help impart backspin, and clubs with extra loft were added; the key was now not simply to make the ball go but also to make it stop.

The ball also turned out to be salvo number one in an endless battle between technology and golf course design. Hitherto, American golf architecture had been a matter of quantity rather than quality. Equipment maker AG Spalding had dispatched a certain Tom Bendelow across America to serve as architect for anyone who wanted a course. Bendelow had no particular knowledge or training, but he had a Scottish accent and he worked for just $25 per design. He also worked quickly, perpetrating more than 600 courses, most of them mediocre.

But the new and better ball commanded new and better courses, so architects went back to their drawing boards, designing longer layouts and adding thousands of yards to those that existed.

In Pittsburgh, Henry and William Fownes unveiled Oakmont, with long, narrow fairways, more than 200 bunkers and 18 fiercely sloped greens that were maintained at breakneck speed.

With Oakmont, the penal school of golf course architecture was born.

Golf's first top-notch resort course began to take shape when in 1901 Donald Ross emigrated from Royal Dornoch in Scotland to the sandhills of North Carolina and started work on Pinehurst Number 2. At the same time, hotel owner George Crump became obsessed with constructing the world's hardest golf course.

With the aid of English architect Harry Colt, he

created Pine Valley in New Jersey. With every fairway and green set off by sand and scrub, it was a relentless examination in shot making and strategy. When Pine Valley opened in 1913, other designers hailed it as America's finest course, and in many observers' eyes it still is.

Three more Philadelphians would leave indelible marks on golf course design: Albert Tillinghast (mostly in the East, with Winged Foot and Baltusrol

his monuments); George Thomas (a pair of gems at Riviera and the Los Angeles Country Club in Southern California); and Hugh Wilson (a masterpiece at Merion).

New courses were more playable and enjoyable than their predecessors – because of the advent in 1913 of the power mower. Fairways and greens could now be maintained swiftly and meticulously, and golf would never be the same again.

ABOVE The 418 yard par 4, 5th hole with the par 3, 3rd green behind on the East Course at Merion Golf Club

Chapter 4

The Great Triumvirate

Harry Vardon

TO MANY GOLFERS, THE NAME Vardon describes the grip they use, the little finger of the right hand riding piggyback on the forefinger of the left hand. To followers of American professional golf, it's the name on the trophy for the tour's leading player in the stroke averages.

If you place 'Harry' in front of the surname, however, you have one of the most influential characters who ever played the game. Harry Vardon was a golfing pioneer, and his influence was almost revolutionary.

Born in Jersey in 1870, Vardon started caddying at a young age and was smitten by the game. His elder brother turned professional first, but Harry soon followed in his footsteps, and quickly established himself as the superior golfer.

By his early 20s, this elegant swinger was playing like no other golfer. He could fade it, draw it, knock it down or loft it up, but most of all he could hit it straight – very straight.

Vardon's game was all about precision. He was a slimly-built fellow

without the physical presence to overpower a golf course, but he knew how to break down its defences with guile and skill. Driving the ball as straight as he did meant he was more often than not playing shots from the fairway, and he capitalised by becoming a great iron player.

He was a fine putter until his late 30s, by which time he was suffering from the

ABOVE
Portrait of Harry
Varden, taken in 1907

OPPOSITE
Spectators on their way
to the 18th green at
Gleneagles

since Old Tom Morris in 1867. Roberto de Vicenzo, victor in 1967, is the only man to win an Open in its present format at an older age than Vardon – and then by only 51 days.

The 1900 US Open in Chicago was a defining moment for Vardon. He already had three Open Championships to his credit and three more would come over the next 14 years. But this was his opportunity to make his mark in front of a new audience, and he seized it.

Vardon won with a display of patient, precision golf that lent something of an inevitable air to his game – a characteristic that opponents could find dispiriting. Vardon wasn't one for animated gestures or shouting about his talents, but his gifts

'yips'. Not that he let it stop him winning tournaments: Vardon's grit easily matched his physical skills.

He won the 1914 Open Championship at the age of 44 years and 42 days, the oldest man to do so

were there for all to see in his shots and, in his prime, he was unshakeable mentally. He was, without a shadow of a doubt, the world's best golfer at that time.

He went on to play in two more US Opens, and he finished second on both occasions. The second of those

runner-up spots was when he was a 50, not in good health but still talented enough to hold a four-shot lead with seven holes to play. In his heyday, it would have been unthinkable for Vardon to let the title slip through his fingers. But he was weakened by illness and that ultimately proved his undoing. His major winning days were over, but what a time he'd had of it.

James Braid

DURING VARDON'S PLAYING career, only two players in Britain could give him more than a decent game: sturdy fellow Englishman JH Taylor, and bushy-moustached Scot James Braid. For the best part of 20 years, the trio dominated the game and became known as 'The Great Triumvirate'.

Braid, a popular, colourful character, was tall and powerful, an awesome hitter, with big hands and an aggressive swing. He wasn't the straightest of hitters but that wasn't a problem, because Braid had a very fine touch around the greens.

Born just down the road from St Andrews, Braid was from a poor family and golf did not find him easily. However, he soon developed into a fine player, although he was the last of the Great Triumvirate to hit the big time.

But Braid was soon winning major trophies like a man in a hurry. Before he had won his first Open, Harry Vardon had three to his name. And yet Braid was the first man to win five Opens, in an extraordinary 10-year spell.

Braid was exciting to watch, with the same attacking style employed later by Arnold Palmer and Seve Ballesteros. Galleries relished the fact that one never

BELOW The 6th hole at
St Enodoc Golf Club

knew what was coming next, but it was invariably worth watching.

Braid became the first club professional at Walton Heath in Surrey and was also a prolific designer, responsible for dozens of courses all over Britain. His legacy lives on in such classic layouts as the King's Course at Gleneagles, St Enodoc in Cornwall and Blairgowrie Rosemount in Scotland.

BELOW The 6th hole at St Enodoc Golf Club

JH Taylor

BEFORE BRAID CAME ON THE scene, JH Taylor was Vardon's greatest rival. Indeed, he was something of a young prodigy, winning a couple of Open Championships before Vardon had opened his account.

Taylor, who grew up playing on the links of Westward Ho! in Devon, had a tidy, compact swing and his speciality was low, punchy iron shots. He was sturdy, with a low centre of gravity and excellent balance, and had the qualities to play great golf in windy conditions.

Taylor thrived on the Open's windswept links courses, and he had the ideal temperament to go with his all-round game. Remaining calm

ABOVE John Henry Taylor playing a shot during the British Open at St Andrews

at all times gave him the ability to choose the right shots under pressure, and he knew how to grasp a winning opportunity.

It was no surprise when Taylor fired a record first-round 75 in the 1893 Open at Prestwick. He failed to win that year, but that supreme round was a taste of things to come.

RIGHT From the left: John H Taylor, James Braid, Harry Vardon and Fred Herd

At the next Open, at Sandwich, he became the first Englishman to win the championship, on the first occasion the event was held outside Scotland. When the championship returned to St Andrews the following year, Taylor won it again. Twelve months later at Muirfield, he was within a whisker of a hat-trick but, having tied with Vardon after 72 holes, he lost the two-round playoff. Nevertheless, it was the start of an impressive Open sequence for Taylor.

Perhaps his finest achievement was at the 1900 Open at St Andrews, where he produced the lowest score in every round and left Braid and Vardon trailing. That same year he came close in the US Open, but was pipped by Vardon.

Taylor designed many fine courses, including his beloved Royal Mid Surrey, where he became the pro, and Datchet, near Windsor. He also helped elevate the status of his fellow professionals.

He was a speaker of high regard, articulate and much in demand for public engagements. And he is regarded as the man most responsible for setting up the fledgling Professional Golfers Association.

Chapter 5

The Ultimate Amateur

Bobby Jones

HE WAS ONLY 14 WHEN HE BURST on the scene in the 1916 US Amateur at Merion, but Robert Tyre Jones Jnr was already well known in his native Georgia. A year earlier he had shot a course-record 68 at the East Lake Country Club in Atlanta, where he had been club champion at age 12. And two weeks before heading north, he had beaten men twice his age to become Georgia State Amateur Champion.

At Merion, Jones made his way through two matches before losing to defending champion Bob Gardner, while captivating everyone with his long drives, crisp irons and fearless assault on the course.

In those days, Jones's only weakness was his temper. Prone to fits of extreme anger, he cursed like a docker and threw clubs at the smallest provocation. In time, he learned to control his fire, and there then flourished a grand career.

From 1923 to 1930, Jones won four US Opens, three British Opens, five US Amateurs and one British Amateur – a total of 13 national championships. Of his last 12 Opens – nine US, three British – he

compiled it while playing no more often than the average duffer.

An amateur to the core, he put his family first, then his law business, and finally golf. He hated practice and some years the only tournaments he played were the national championships he won.

Jones was a supremely natural player who swept serenely through the ball with a rhythmic swing whose lazy grace belied its power. His tee shots averaged 250 yards and for decades he was the only man ever to get home in two at the par five, 603-yard 17th hole of the Olympic Club in San Francisco. But Jones's true strengths were his surgically accurate irons and his touch with Calamity Jane, his simple blade putter.

won seven, and in four of the other five he was runner-up. No other player has come close to matching this phenomenal record – and Jones

Jones had already established himself as the best golfer in the world when, in 1930, he did the unthinkable, winning

ABOVE Bobby Jones practising his swing on the roof of the Savoy Hotel in London

the Open and Amateur titles of America and Great Britain in one season.

It was a journey that began in St Andrews with the title Jones wanted most, the British Amateur. In three of a gruelling series of eight matches, Bobby squeezed through by 1-up. In the 36-hole final against England's Roger Wethered, he won by seven holes up with six to play.

Two weeks later, at Hoylake, Jones broke the competitive course record for 72 holes and won his third British Open by two strokes. No American had ever won both titles, and New Yorkers gave him a ticker-tape welcome home.

At the US Open at Interlachen, a 68 in round three gave him a five-stroke lead. In the final round, Jones double-bogeyed three of the four par–3 holes but, in a trademark display of resilience, finished with birdies on three of his last six holes for a two-stroke victory.

His victory in the US Amateur at Merion seemed pre-ordained. Jones was never down to an opponent and, in the 36-hole final, beat Eugene Homans by eight up with seven to play.

Bobby Jones was the epitome of modesty and grace, a Southern gentle-man, revered above all of America's sportsmen, yet humble. At Harvard, he was ineligible for the golf team, having already played at Georgia Tech so, at a time when he was US Open Champion, he served as the team's assistant manager. And his name was so synonymous with perfect behaviour that the USGA named its highest award for sportsmanship after him.

But his career was as brief as it was brilliant. Jones was only 28 when he completed the Grand Slam – and at that point, having achieved all of his goals, he retired.

BELOW Bobby Jones on the right with fellow competitor Gene Sarazen on the left

He had plenty to keep him occupied. He published books, designed clubs for Spalding and collaborated with Warner Brothers on a series of instructional film shorts co-starring the likes of Jimmy Cagney and Edward G Robinson. But most of Jones's energy went into the pursuit of a dream.

In 1931 he and a group of investors purchased 365 acres near Augusta, Georgia, and in January 1933 the Augusta National opened for play.

The site offered rolling countryside planted with a dazzling assortment of trees, shrubs and flowers, with Georgia pines, azaleas and dogwoods prominent. Scottish architect Alister Mackenzie – whose designs include Australia's Royal Melbourne and Cypress Point in California, a 1928 creation considered to be among the world's top 10 courses – collaborated with Jones on the design.

Jones had two desires: that the course rise out of the terrain rather than be stamped on it, recalling the rolling feel of Scottish linksland; and that each hole offer alternative lines of attack, with the reward in proportion to the risk.

Augusta National's generous fairways, sparse bunkering and expansive greens gave it a wide-open, welcoming appearance. It looked easy but wasn't – exactly what Jones wanted.

After Augusta National opened, the USGA expressed interest in holding a US Open there, but the idea did not sit well with the club members. "If we're going to hold a tournament," they reasoned, "let's hold our own."

So in 1934 The Masters was born, with Jones as host. In those days it was called The Augusta National Invitation: an invitation from Jones to old compatriots and the best new players. But it became something more when Jones was persuaded to come out of retirement and play. But his chipping and putting were not what the public had hoped for, however, and he finished the tournament in a tie for 13th place.

Nowhere did Jones enrapture fans more than at St Andrews. It was here that much of his career unfolded, from his first Open appearance in 1921 – when poor play led him to stomp off the course – to the Open he dominated from start to finish in 1927, and his crowning achievement in the Amateur of 1930.

In 1936 he returned to the Old

ABOVE Bobby Jones putting at the Amateur Golf Championship at Hoylake, 1921

ABOVE Bobby Jones holding the trophy after winning the 1927 Open Golf Championship at St Andrews

Course, unannounced, for a casual round. By the time he reached the first tee, 5,000 St Andreans were waiting to see him play. More than 20 years passed before Jones returned again, and when he did he was made a Freeman of the Royal Burgh of St Andrews.

Bobby Jones died in 1971, leaving a legacy like no other. His spirit lives on every year in the Masters, an event that has grown in leaps and bounds since 1934.

Gene Sarazen

AND THE BIGGEST LEAP CAME one year after its inception, when Gene Sarazen fired "the shot heard round the world".

Sarazen was three strokes off the lead in the final round when he came to the 15th hole, a 500-yard par five. After his tee shot left him 230 yards from the hole, he elected to go for the green with a 4-wood.

The ball shot out low and straight at the flag, cleared the pond in front of the green, took one big bounce and rolled straight into the cup for an albatross 2. Sarazen had made up all three strokes with one shot. He went on to par the last three holes and tie with Craig Wood, whom he trounced in a playoff.

Suddenly, the tournament had tradition and panache. Today, The Masters ranks with the Open, US Open and the PGA Championship as one of the four most coveted titles in golf. With his dramatic victory, Sarazen became the first man to win all four.

The son of Italian immigrants, Sarazen had learned the game as a caddie in suburban New York. In 1922,

his name was etched on to the US Open trophy when Sarazen won by one stroke over Jones. Later that summer, at 20, he became the youngest PGA champion ever and in 1923 he made it two PGAs in a row.

But the success may have been too much too soon, and he fell into a decade

BELOW Bobby Jones playing a mashie shot during the British Open Golf Championship at St Andrews, 1927

BELOW Gene Sarazen in action

of relative decline. In 1932, Sarazen decided his high scores had come largely from poor bunker play – so he invented the sand wedge.

Sarazen got his idea while flying: when the tail fins went down, the plane rose. Reasoning that if he could lower the sole of his niblick it would help lift the ball from sand, he soldered a thick flange on the back of the club, angled so that the flange hit the sand first, allowing the front of the club to bounce upward. Now he could hit behind the ball and splash it out.

At the Open in 1932 at Sandwich, Sarazen's new club saved him stroke after stroke and he won by five strokes, breaking the 72-hole record. Two weeks later, he won the US Open at Skokie Country Club.

At about the same time, another equipment development was occurring. The USGA and the Royal & Ancient had approved the production of golf clubs with tubular steel shafts. Clubmaking switched from a craft dependent on the skills of artisans to a purely mechanical process, and suddenly all clubs were created equal.

Up to this point, golfers had built up their arsenals haphazardly, buying a brassie here and a mashie there in hopes of assembling a collection of sticks with similar heft and flex. Often, the result was a bagful of weapons at odds with one another. But steel shafts put an end to that with the advent of the matched set. Not only were the clubs consistent, but the lie of the clubhead and the flexibility of the shaft could be tailored to fit individual needs.

It was also at this time that golf clubs began to be designated with numbers instead of names – the spoon became a 3-wood, the mashie a 5-iron, the niblick a 9-iron – and for a while the numbers got out of hand. Lawson Little, the winner of back-to-back titles in the US and British Amateurs in 1934 and 1935, is reputed to have used no fewer than 31 clubs.

Something had to be done, so in 1938 the USGA limited the golfer's armaments to 14. The R&A followed a year later.

Four years later a cap was imposed on the liveliness of the ball. In the 20s, the game's ruling bodies had limited the size and weight of the ball, but that hadn't stopped one manufacturer from creating a rocket that went 50 yards farther than anything on the market.

What's more, as golfers began swinging their steel shafts with a vigour impossible in the hickory era, everyone from tour pros to grandmothers got extra distance. So, in 1942, the USGA imposed a limit on the velocity a golf ball may have at impact, to 250ft per second.

ABOVE Gene Sarazen with the trophy at the British Open Golf Championships at Princes Course, Sandwich 1932

Chapter 6

An American Triumvirate

AS GOLF EQUIPMENT BECAME more consistent, precise and powerful, so did the players, and in the late 1930s a new breed of strong and talented professionals came to the fore. Among them was England's answer to Bobby Jones, the legendary Henry Cotton.

Cotton was a sublime ball-striker, and exceptionally long when he needed to be, because he had reserves of effortless power. This was due partly to good technique, but he was also very strong – one of his favourite drills was hitting 5-iron shots using just his left arm.

Cotton elevated the status of professional golfers, many of whom at that time were treated as second-class citizens: it was common for them not to be allowed in the clubhouse. Cotton would not stand for such nonsense and was not afraid to say as much. But he did not always endear himself to his fellow pros, often preferring not to mix with them. And he had a fiery temperament, kept under wraps during championships but often in evidence off the course.

But Cotton could be generous with his knowledge. In 1938, he travelled to St Andrews at his own expense to advise the Great Britain and Ireland Walker

Cup team. The home side won the Cup for the first time in its history.

Cotton won three Open Championships and his first, in 1934 at Sandwich, was perhaps his finest. Aged just 27, he produced world-class golf that blew everyone else into the weeds. Starting with a 67, he then shot a second-round 65 – a championship record score that stood for 43 years and inspired Dunlop to name the 65 ball. Only five golfers broke 70 in that Open and Cotton shot two of the rounds, giving him an unassailable nine-shot lead.

When he won the championship again in 1937, Cotton was at the height of his powers. He would surely have won several more Opens had the Second World War not intervened, and he had to wait until 1948 for his hat-trick. By then he had turned 40 and knew it would probably be pretty much downhill after that – but he was still capable of winning well into the 1950s. He retired to his beloved Penina golf course in Portugal, where young pros flocked to meet him.

Across the pond, golf got another much-needed shot in the arm when America produced its own Great Triumvirate: Byron Nelson, Sam Snead and Ben Hogan.

LEFT Henry Cotton – who demanded better treatment for golfing professionals and wrote on the subject in newspaper columns and magazines

Byron Nelson

ALL THREE WERE BORN IN 1912, but it was Nelson, a lanky, baby-faced Texan, who first gained major attention when he won the 1937 Masters.

In the final round he was four strokes off the lead of Ralph Guldahl. But at Augusta's par-three 12th, Guldahl took a double-bogey 5, then followed with a bogey at the par-five 13th. Nelson birdied the 12th and eagled the 13th, taking a two-stroke lead that he never relinquished.

Two years later, Nelson won the US Open in dramatic style, holing a 1-iron approach shot for eagle en route to a playoff victory. That iron was not unexpected, for no one since Harry Vardon had hit the ball with the accuracy of Lord Byron.

His key was a swing unlike all others and the first to adapt successfully to the steel-shafted club. While the rest of the world continued to imitate Bobby Jones, with little leg movement and a pivot against a tall and braced left side, Nelson put some action in his legs, let his left knee buckle, and dipped downward through impact. However, he continued to use one element of the Jones swing – the straight left arm.

Until that time, the left arm was allowed to bend on the backswing, to keep players' motion in sync with their wooden-shafted clubs. But if the shafts were firmer, so the leading arm could

ABOVE Byron Nelson competing in a Ryder Cup match at Royal Birkdale, Southport, 1937

be, too. Nelson helped popularise the 'modern' swing, very similar to the one we use today.

By 1944, he had lifted a second Masters, the PGA and two dozen tour victories. In 1944 alone he won eight events, but he was about to climb even higher.

In 1945, Byron Nelson came as close as any golfer has come to being unbeatable. He won 18 of that year's 35 tournaments, 11 of them in one string; he finished second seven times; his scoring average was a phenomenal 68.33; and he finished every tournament under par.

At the end of the next season, with most of his ambitions fulfilled, Nelson retired and bought a Texas cattle ranch. Years later, he returned to the game as a TV commentator and host of the Byron Nelson Classic tournament.

Samuel Snead

WHEN NELSON RETIRED IN 1946, aged 34, Samuel Jackson Snead was just getting warmed up. Although by 1945 he had three dozen victories under his belt, there were nearly 50 more wins ahead of him in a career that would last another 34 years and beyond.

Slammin' Sam came out of western Virginia with more raw talent than the game had ever seen and with a swing as strong and graceful as the leap of a panther. In his first pro event, the 1936 Hershey Open, Sam belted two opening drives out of bounds. For his third attempt, he let his swing flow and drove the green, 350 yards away. With that shot, he arrived.

Snead won his first event later that year and the next year he won five more, the first instalments in a total of 84 victories – more than any man in history.

But in that same 1937 season, Snead finished second in the US Open despite a four-round total of 283, just one stroke off the tournament record. The only blemish on his career is his failure to win the US Open despite 37 tries, a dozen top-ten finishes and four times as runner-up.

Snead's most painful loss was to Byron Nelson in 1939 at the Spring Mill Country Club near Philadelphia, where a par five on his final hole would have

taken the title. Thinking he needed a birdie, Snead stumbled to an eight.

He had another chance in 1947 at St Louis Country Club where, in a playoff with Lew Worsham, the two came to the 18th green still even and with both balls about 30in from the cup. Snead set up to putt first, but Worsham asked for a ruling. "That kind of rattled me," Snead said. He was, indeed, farther away, and

ABOVE Sam Snead at Carnoustie in Scotland, 1937

round one shot behind Hogan; a final-round 76 left him six back.

But Snead recovered both his composure and his game. No entry in the record book is longer than his: among his seven dozen wins are three Masters, three PGAs and the 1946 Open, plus scores of lesser titles.

Age never seemed to slow Snead. In 1965 he won the Greater Greensboro becoming, at 52 years and 10 months, the oldest player ever to win on the USPGA Tour. And he tied for third in the 1974 USPGA Championship – at the age of 62!

But his competitive days were far from over. When in 1980 he won the Commemorative, a Senior event, he became the first golfer to record victories in six different decades.

Ben Hogan

WHILE SNEAD PLAYED GOLF naturally, Ben Hogan had to "dig it out of the dirt". Just 5ft 8½ in and under 10 stone, Hogan was the runt of the caddie pen at the Glen Garden Country Club near Fort Worth, where Byron Nelson also learned the game.

when he putted, he missed. Worsham made, for a one-stroke win.

In 1949, at Medinah, Snead needed pars on the last two holes but took three strokes from the edge of the 17th. And in 1953 at Oakmont, he entered the final

In 1927, Bantam Ben lost the caddie championship to Nelson – and did not enjoy his first taste of defeat.

But there was more frustration to come. For the first several years of his career he fought a vicious hook, and he made three abortive attempts at the pro circuit before achieving modest success in 1937. It was another three years before he broke through with his first victory at the Pinehurst North-South. By that time, Nelson and Snead had won 30 tournaments.

But Hogan won in each of the two weeks following Pinehurst, taking four tournaments in all, and finished the season as the leading money winner. In 1941 and 1942 he continued the domination, piling up a dozen more victories.

Hogan served two years in the Army Air Corps before his discharge in the summer of 1945. Once back, he wasted no time, winning five events by the end of the year. Then, in 1946, he put together a season nearly as overpowering as Nelson's in 1945: of the 32 events he entered, Hogan won 13, finished second in six and third in three.

Among the tournaments he won was his first major championship – the USPGA – and among those he almost won were The Masters and the US Open. In both of those two, a missed putt at the final hole cost him the title.

Hogan was never able to master the putting game, but he came as close as

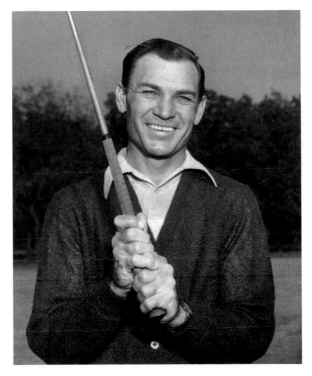

BELOW The legendary Ben Hogan smiles while holding a golf club

anyone to mastering golf from tee to green. He claimed he preferred practice to play and, through relentless pursuit of improvement, banished his hook in favour of a fade.

In 1947, Hogan again led the Tour in victories with seven, and in 1948 he added 10 more, including a second USPGA Championship and his first US Open. Eight months later, he was lucky to be alive. In February, his car collided head-on with a Greyhound bus and he broke a collarbone, fractured his pelvis, crushed an ankle and suffered massive internal injuries.

Doctors said he might never walk again, but by August Hogan was

swinging a club and by December he was on the course. The following January he returned to the site of his US Open victory, Riviera, for a comeback. Incredibly, he shot 73-69-69-69, and appeared to have won before Sam Snead tied him and then prevailed in a playoff.

At the US Open at Merion, visibly in pain from walking a 36-hole final day, he managed to tie Lloyd Mangrum and George Fazio in regulation play, then beat them the next day in an 18-hole playoff.

Thereafter, Hogan concentrated on the majors, winning his first Masters in 1951 and in the same year taking the US Open at Oakland Hills, over a set-up considered the most severe test ever.

But Hogan's vintage year was 1953, during which he won the Masters, the US Open and the British Open inside 12 weeks. At Augusta, he won with a 284 that lowered the tournament record by five. At Oakmont, he led from wire to wire to take the US Open. Then, persuaded to play the Open for the first time, he spent a week learning about linksland golf and assaulted the course at Carnoustie. With a course-record 68 in the final round, he won by four strokes and became the first player to

win the Masters and the US and British Opens in the same year.

Hogan won nine major championships, and his name remains a symbol of courage, dedication and indomitable spirit. And for many golfers it also means hope – of improving their swing. For years, there were rumours of a 'secret', and in 1955, Hogan confessed to Life magazine that he 'cupped' the left wrist just before reaching the top of the backswing.

In 1957, in Five Lessons: The Modern Fundamentals of Golf, written with Herbert Warren Wind, he described the 'pronation' of the wrists as well as the importance of the left hip turning out of the way on the downswing to generate power. And he introduced a new image: he visualised a pane of glass that ran from the ball up through the shoulders and indicated the proper plane of the swing. His ideas are still being debated, and tried.

ABOVE Ben Hogan plays a tee shot as the gallery looks on during the 4th annual International Golf Contest for the Canada Cup at Wentworth

Chapter 7

The Ladies' Game

NEW SILK :: SPORTS COATS

Registered design (as sketch), the most useful garment imaginable, beautifully made from rich quality, double-combed silk, extra bright finish, combining the fit of a perfectly made tailor coat with the comfort and warmth of a throw-on. A dainty and most becoming garment, stocked in more than 100 fashionable shades.

33 inches long,	63/-
36 " "	72/6
44 " "	94/6
Silk cap to match,	21/-

SENT ON APPROVAL.

Debenham & Freebody
Wigmore Street
(Cavendish Sq.), London. W.
Famous over a Century for Taste, for Quality, for Value.

ABOVE An advertisement for women's golfing fashions, 1910

EVER SINCE MARY Queen of Scots, women all over the world have embraced the game of golf. It wasn't until the mid-19th century, however, that the first ladies' clubs were formed.

At that time, restrictive clothing made it impossible for women to exploit their talents fully. It was even considered unladylike to swing the club above shoulder height, and the women's game was unlikely to take off in a big way. Things changed, though. The Ladies' Golf Union was formed in 1893 and by the early 1900s, women's golf was in good health on both sides of the Atlantic.

But it was not very profitable. While the era of Ben Hogan, Byron Nelson and Sam Snead transformed big-time golf into a game strictly for professionals, the top women players remained amateur until after the Second World War. This is not to say that there weren't some very fine women golfers. Two were downright magnificent.

During the 1920s, Joyce Wethered ruled Britannia with a graceful, compact swing and a buoyant temperament. In one incident at Sheringham, she putted out while a train thundered past 30 feet away. After securing victory, she was asked if the train hadn't put her off. Her reply: "what train?"

Wethered won four British Amateurs

Joyce Wethered in front of the St Andrews golf course clubhouse in 1929

and five consecutive English Amateurs before retiring at 28. Bobby Jones called her the finest golfer – man or woman – he had ever seen.

Her last British Amateur title, in 1929, came with a 2-up victory over the other powerhouse of women's golf, America's Glenna Collett. No woman in

the US was a match for Glenna, who dominated the US Amateur with a record six victories, including three in a row from 1928–30, along with dozens of lesser events.

Her single frustration was in never winning the British Amateur, but when Margaret and Harriott Curtis, a pair of former US Amateur Champions from Boston, donated a cup for competition between America and Great Britain & Ireland, Glenna got a measure of satisfaction. The Curtis Cup was born, and Glenna was on the first six, undefeated US teams.

The 1946 US Amateur and 1947 British Amateur titles went to a Texan woman who changed the face of women's golf. Her name was Mildred, but everyone knew her as Babe.

Babe Didrikson was famous before she found celebrity as a golfer. She won gold in the javelin and 80-metre hurdles at the 1932 Olympics, and she was gifted at everything she tried: basketball, swimming, diving, rifle shooting, bowling, figure skating, bike racing and tennis. She even dabbled in baseball and football. But golf became her true love, and it soon outshone all her other sporting achievements combined.

The first formal round she played, she shot 93 while slugging out 250-yard tee shots. In 1935, she won the first important tournament she entered, the Texas Women's Amateur Championship.

Babe brought a new work ethic to women's golf: learning from Tommy Armour, the finest teacher of the time, she played and practised up to 16 hours a day. Her first years were spent touring in exhibitions with top men professionals, and later with her husband, professional wrestler George Zaharias. A born entertainer, when asked how a slender woman of 5 foot 7 could hit the ball so far, she said, "I just hitch up my girdle and give it a rip."

Her exhibitions made her a professional in the eyes of the USGA, but by 1944 she was reinstated as an amateur and wasted no time in winning the 1946 US Women's Amateur and the 1947 British Amateur at Gullane.

The Babe then turned pro again, and made the astute decision to acquire the services of agent Fred Corcoran. That same year, she signed a contract with Wilson Sporting Goods for $100,000.

But what the Babe really wanted was serious competition and an audience. So in 1950, the Ladies Professional Golf Association was formed in the US, with 11 women as its charter members. Corcoran stage-managed the tour and Wilson paid the bills, but the women kept the books, handled the

BELOW Portrait of Babe Didrikson Zaharias posing on a golf course

Babe Didrickson Zaharias

BELOW Babe Didrikson Zaharias putting the ball, mid 1940s

correspondence and called their own rulings.

The Babe dominated the early years, racking up an astonishing 31 tournament victories. And she likely would have won dozens more events had her career not been curtailed by cancer.

She was diagnosed in 1953, but a mere fourteen weeks later she was back on the course, and the next year she won five tournaments. Three more victories came in 1955, but then the cancer returned. In 1956, Babe Zaharias died at the tragically young age of 42.

But Babe was not the only talent on that fledgling women's tour. Even on her best days, she could be beaten by the freckle-faced Patty Berg.

By the age of 16, Patty had won the Minneapolis City Golf Championship and a year later she nearly won the US Amateur, a title she later went on to claim along with 28 others.

During the War she served in the women's Marines, then came out firing as a professional golfer with a victory in the first Women's US Open in 1946. Along with Babe, Berg – who was the LPGA's first President – dominated women's pro golf for the next decade, amassing 44 wins.

The two other top-notch players at the dawn of the LPGA were Louise Suggs and Betsy Rawls. Suggs developed

Open four times – Mickey Wright.

She finished fourth in her first Open, in 1954, but in the decade that followed, Mickey Wright set a new standard in women's pro golf. Shy and retiring, she delivered in game what she lacked in glamour, with a swing that is to this day called the finest golf has produced.

From 1957 until 1965 there was no one who could touch Mickey. Over that span she won 65 tournaments, nearly a third of those she entered. In 1961, she won ten events including

such clubhead speed that people called her the female Ben Hogan. Before turning pro she won the US and British Amateurs, then added two US Opens and an LPGA Championship, among 50 career victories.

Rawls joined the tour in 1951, won her first US Open the same year and added 54 other events. Only one other player has won the Women's US

reflected the good times. After two decades of depression and war, new courses were popping up everywhere in the US and Britain. They weren't quite like the old ones.

Earth-moving equipment had replaced horse-drawn scrapers and riding mowers had made courses easier to maintain, while also producing mammoth greens and tees.

The prominent architects of the '20s and '30s had passed away, but into the breach had stepped Robert Trent Jones. A fine amateur player, Jones became the first man to train specifically as a golf course architect. At Cornell University he devised his own curriculum, combining landscape design and agronomy, and it was he who, in 1993, designed the LPGA's home course at Daytona, Florida.

the US Open, the LPGA Championship and her own Mickey Wright Open in her hometown of San Diego. She followed with ten more wins in 1962, a record 13 in 1963 and 11 in 1964.

The rise of Mickey Wright mirrored the growth of the LPGA, which in turn

Mickey Wright's retirement had left a void in women's golf. But one discovery was Texan Kathy Whitworth, who led the LPGA money list eight times between 1965 and 1973. No player has amassed more official victories than

Whitworth, who totalled 88 wins and became the first woman golfer to pass one million dollars in official prize winnings.

In a similar milestone to Whitworth's, American Judy Rankin broke the $100,000 barrier for a single season when in 1976 she won seven events.

Then there was long-hitting JoAnne Carner. She didn't turn pro until she was 30, but in the

decade and half starting in 1970, she won 42 LPGA titles, while adding a dash of colour to women's golf.

In 1975, New York marketing mogul Ray Volpe took over as Commissioner of the LPGA, and under his seven-year leadership the tour's purses quadrupled and the televised events jumped from two to 14. More talented women began joining the LPGA Tour.

One of them, Nancy Lopez from New Mexico, became the LPGA's first

LEFT USA captain JoAnne Carner holds the trophy after victory in the Solheim Cup at the Greenbrier in White Sulphur Springs, West Virginia, USA in October 1994

ABOVE Nancy Lopez in action

remained the LPGA Tour's marquee attraction for 20 years. But at the same time, the supporting cast became stronger as players such as Pat Bradley, Beth Daniel, Amy Alcott, Patty Sheehan and Betsy King took women's pro golf to a new level.

The LPGA began billing itself "the best women golfers in the world", and today Sweden's Annika Sorenstam is the dominant player in a tour that has expanded to include events in Canada, England, Australia, Japan and South Korea.

She may well be joined by Hawaii-born six-footer Michelle Wie, who tied for ninth place in the first major championship of 2003 – when she was just 13.

Nothing can prepare you for the shock of seeing Wie hit a golf ball. Receiving a special invitation to play in the Sony Open in Hawaii in 2004, her tee shots matched the average distance of the entire field. In the short time since then, Michelle has become the youngest golfer in Curtis Cup history, left an impressive mark on several men's PGA Tour events, finished second in two LPGA major events and left folk wondering just how far she can go. And this has all happened to a young

superstar, with a phenomenal rookie year. She scored back-to-back early-season victories, and then won the next five events she entered – including the LPGA Championship. That season, Lopez won nine times and established a new scoring average.

From there she just got better, winning 50 tournaments, and Lopez

woman who was born as late as 1989.

Women's golf in Europe experienced difficult times in the '80s and '90s, but it is now capitalising on the success of some of the continent's finest players –

who also happen to be some of the world's best.

For years the Women's British Open struggled to assert itself, until finally it was awarded major status. With that came big prize money, and the Women's British Open is assured of a world-class gathering of talent every year.

As is Solheim Cup week. This event, launched in 1990, is essentially the women's equivalent of the Ryder Cup, contested biennially between the leading professionals in Europe and the United States.

Thirty or 40 years ago, the tournament – named after Karsten Solheim, the founder of the Ping golf company – might have been a walkover for the US. As it was, its launch coincided with a period when European golf was thriving as never before.

In Laura Davies, Europe has one of the world's best

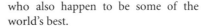

LEFT Laura Davies celebrates after she birdies at the second hole during the Solheim Cup at the Dalmahoy Golf Club in Scotland, 1992

golfers – and certainly the most exciting to watch. Her hero is Seve Ballesteros, so it's no coincidence that she plays like him. She exploded on to the scene in the mid-1980s, thumping drives in a fashion that set her apart from any other golfer of her generation.

There is no greater treat than watching Davies unleash a drive with seemingly no regard for the consequences. To go with the power, though, she has a strong all-round game and a courageous, fighting spirit.

Having played in the 1984 Curtis Cup, Laura turned pro and promptly won her first tournament, the Belgian Open. That season she was Rookie of the Year and in 1987 she was for a while the holder of both the US and British Open titles.

While Laura was still at her inspired best, along came the contrasting persona of Sweden's Annika Sorenstam. Her diminutive frame and unassuming manner hides one of the greatest women's golf talents of all time. Quiet, softly spoken, but a clinical winning machine, Annika was leading individual in the 1992 World Amateur Team Championship and blitzed the collegiate world while at the University of Arizona.

After turning pro, she won the Rookie of the Year title in 1993 in Europe and claimed the same title in the US in 1995, a year in which she became the first player to top the European and LPGA Tour money lists in the same season. That year she also won her first US Open.

Sorenstam can produce explosive streaks of low scoring, yet she does not suffer the dips in form that so many

golfers endure. There isn't another golfer, male or female, who makes fewer mistakes than Annika.

She has a good technique and swings the club with a beautiful, smooth rhythm. She hits almost every fairway and green and she putts like an angel. To cap it all, she has an unflappable, nerveless disposition.

Can Annika match Kathy Whitworth's record number of official wins of 88? She shows every sign of being able to do so, having already notched up close to 70 victories and continuing her spree in 2006 with a win in the US Women's Open.

Together, Annika and Laura spearheaded Europe's challenge in the early years of the Solheim Cup. The inaugural contest in 1990, at Lake Nona in Florida, witnessed a powerful performance from the United States. But two years later at Dalmahoy in Scotland, Europe turned the tables. Leading by one point after the first two days, the home side routed the supposedly stronger Americans in the singles matches by 7-3.

Like the men's professional game, women's golf has changed beyond all recognition in the last 100 years. But it's never looked in better health.

LEFT Annika Sorenstam holds the winner's trophy for the 1996 US Women's Open Championship

Chapter 8

The Big Three

TO MOST PEOPLE, THE NAME OF George S May does not mean a thing in the context of golf's Big Three – Arnold Palmer, Jack Nicklaus and Gary Player. But this flamboyant Chicago businessman played a pivotal role: he launched the era of televised golf.

And what a moment May chose to put golf on TV. In 1953, for the final round of the World Championship of Golf, he positioned a single camera atop the grandstand at the 18th green of the Tam O'Shanter Country Club. Lew Worsham needed a birdie three to reach a playoff for the record $25,000 first prize and faced a wedge approach of 120 yards. His low shot hit well short of the pin but rolled and rolled – nearly 60 feet – and dropped in for an eagle two and outright victory.

That magic moment, witnessed by a million viewers, changed everything. The US Open came to TV in 1954, the Masters in 1955, and by the early '60s every significant tournament was either on screen or trying to get there.

Arnold Palmer

GOLF'S FIRST TV STAR MADE HIS entrance in the form of Western Pennsylvania's Arnold Daniel Palmer: the classic American hero, with a swaggering gait, a ready smile and the shoulders of an NFL fullback.

Arnold was three when he first picked up a club. At seven he broke a hundred, at 14 he shot 71, and by the time he entered Wake Forest University he had won just about every school, county and state-wide event.

LEFT A portrait of
Arnold Palmer taken in
1953

but he rapped it home from everywhere. He had a burning will to win and the perfect psyche for golf – a fighting spirit without a temper. His go-for-broke style sometimes put him in trouble, but his resourcefulness usually got him out. He didn't play a golf course; he beat it into submission.

A victory in the 1954 US Amateur persuaded him to turn pro, and four years later he won the first of four Masters titles along with four other events. But it was in 1960 that Arnold Palmer truly began his reign.

That April he arrived at Augusta with four wins in his pocket. A first-round 67 gave him the Masters lead, and he held on to it until the final moments on Sunday, when Ken Venturi pulled in front. Palmer came to the last two holes needing two birdies to win, and he got them both. The Palmer Charge was born.

The Palmer swing was less than elegant, but he pulverised the ball. His putting was equally ungraceful, Charge was born.

Six weeks later it became legendary. By the start of the final round of the US

BELOW Arnold Palmer celebrates after sinking a long putt

Open at the Cherry Hills Country Club, he was seven strokes off the lead. But at the par-4 first, Palmer drove the green, 346 yards away. Then his two-putt birdie ignited the most explosive stretch of sub-par golf the US Open had seen – four birdies in a row, six in the first seven holes – for an outward-nine score of 30. Suddenly, Arnie was tied for the lead, and he closed with a seven-under-par 65 for a two-stroke victory.

When Arnie was happy, he grinned; when he was unhappy, he grimaced – and fans celebrated and suffered with him. They celebrated four Masters and they suffered three playoff losses in the US Open. They celebrated back-to-back victories in the Open Championship and they suffered as he struggled to win the USPGA.

In all, Arnold Palmer won 60 US events, and another 29 around the world. He led the money list four times, was the first player to win $100,000 in a single season and the first to reach a million dollars in career earnings. And no player has been loved so much by so many.

Between 1960 and 1970, golf boomed in the United States. The number of players doubled from five million to ten, and the number of courses exploded from 6,300 to 10,000. But no aspect of the game grew more dramatically

The growth did not come without pain. For a time, a conflict brewed between the PGA of America, the sponsors and the players over who should receive the lion's share of broadcast fees. So the players split from their teaching-pro brethren in the PGA, taking most of the rights money with them. USGA executive director Joseph C Dey took over as the first Commissioner of the organisation that became known as the PGA Tour. In 1958, the total purse for the tour had been one million dollars. A decade later, when the PGA Tour was formed, the purses increased to five million.

LEFT Arnold Palmer playing at Wentworth in 1971

BELOW Arnold Palmer looks to line up his putt during the Open Championship, 1981

than the professional tour.

Except for the major championships and a couple of California pro-ams, the tour had for years been a succession of modest, community-run tournaments. But as TV networks and sponsors began to pay serious money, pro golf became big business.

Jack Nicklaus

BELOW Jack Nicklaus plays a majestic iron shot

THAT ERA PRODUCED A LEGION of talented young players, but one rose above them all: Jack Nicklaus.

BELOW Jack Nicklaus plays a majestic iron shot

When he came to golf, the chunky 10-year-old from Columbus, Ohio had, in Charlie Nicklaus, a devoted father who loved the game; in Scioto Country Club, a home course that had hosted a US Open; and in club pro Jack Grout, one of the finest instructors.

But most of all, Jack Nicklaus had raw talent. He shot 51 for the first nine holes he played. By 13 he had broken 70 at Scioto, and at 16 he won the Ohio State Open.

Jack's first step toward immortality came in the 1959 US Amateur Championship, where he scored an 18th-hole victory in the final match. Two years later he won the Amateur and NCAA titles, and the year after that he joined the pro tour.

No player was more eagerly anticipated, and yet none was more rudely greeted. They called him Fat Jack and Nick Louse, said he was too young, too heavy, too sombre, too slow – but the truth was, he wasn't Arnold Palmer.

Where Palmer warmed to the

country, the man treated Arnie's Army to four days of gallant golf. His 283 put him in first place – in a tie with Nicklaus. In the playoff, Jack took the lead at the first hole, never let go and was ahead by three strokes at the end.

He won twice more before the end of that year, then in 1963 exploded for five wins, including the Masters and the USPGA. The 23-year-old Nicklaus remained the man to beat for the next quarter century.

Jack managed his practice and play to peak for the Masters, the US Open, the Open and the USPGA. When he won the 1966 Open he became, at 26, the youngest man to complete the career Grand Slam. And that was just the beginning.

Ultimately, Nicklaus won 18 major championships – six Masters, five USPGAs, four US Opens and three Opens – a record that no other player has approached. He did not simply win; he won in commanding, occasionally

LEFT Jack Nicklaus takes a swing during the Open Golf Championship at Royal Lytham & St Annes in Lancashire, 1969

galleries, Nicklaus ignored them. While Palmer could turn an ordinary round into high drama, Jack made superb play look matter-of-fact. His drives were gargantuan, his irons majestic and he putted with the touch of an angel, but he went about his business with plodding monotony.

The inevitable Palmer-Nicklaus showdown came halfway through Jack's rookie year, in the US Open at Oakmont. In the heart of Palmer

BELOW
Jack Nicklaus and
his wife Barbara
pose with the trophy
for winning the Open
Championship, 1970

superhuman style. His victory in the '65 Masters came by nine strokes with a then-record score of 271.

At one time or another, Nicklaus held or shared the 18-hole and 72-hole scoring records for each of the four major championships. Five times he won two majors in the same year, and in 1972 he came within a whisker of duplicating Ben Hogan's Triple Crown.

But Nicklaus didn't always have it all his own way. Lee Trevino, with six majors, was one of a handful of players who were able occasionally to put a dent in his challenge.

A world-class ball striker and effervescent character, Trevino won only two Open Championships, but he won them back to back. At Birkdale in 1971, he held his nerve on the back nine to edge out Nicklaus. The next year at Muirfield, Trevino succeeded in stopping Nicklaus in his tracks.

Gary Player

A MORE ENDURING CHALLENGE than Trevino's came from the Man in Black: Gary Player, the South African who in the 1960s ranked alongside Nicklaus and Palmer.

No golfer has won more events worldwide – 184 at the last count. Nine of those wins are majors, and when he won the 1965 US Open at Hazeltine, Player joined Hogan and Sarazen in a club that would soon include Nicklaus, as the only players to complete a

performance that he could afford a double-bogey six on the final hole.

Perhaps the greatest of his Open wins involved a classic battle with Nicklaus at Carnoustie in 1968. The fairway wood shot Player hit over bunkers on the par-5 14th to within two feet of the hole, giving him an eagle-three, was one of the most timely shots in championship history.

When he won his second USPGA title at Oakland Hills, Player thumped his ball out of thick rough to within tapping-in distance. It was executed at exactly the right time, and is considered one of the greatest ever wedge shots.

At times, Player could charge just as well as Arnold Palmer – never more evident than at the 1978 Masters. Aged 43, he was trailing the leaders by some distance going into the final round, but he dug deep and birdied seven of his final ten holes for an astonishing

modern Grand Slam of victories. Tiger Woods has since joined them.

Gary Player was the template on which the modern golfer is based, eating bananas when virtually everyone else was smoking and pumping weights when everyone else thought he was mad. And he had a great temperament – gutsy, determined and able to get the job done when it mattered.

Player won Open Championships in three different decades. His first, at Muirfield in 1959, was such a dominant eight-under-par 64 that took the title by one stroke.

That summed up Player's attitude: there was no such thing as a lost cause. In his semi-final against Tony Lema in the 1965 World Matchplay Championship, Player came back from seven down at halfway to tie after 36 holes, and win on the first playoff hole.

Player, the originator of the phrase "the more I practise, the luckier I get", wasn't lucky at all. He had great skill and,

while not possessing a flawless technique, he was immensely strong and made the best of his talent. He was a fine mid-iron player and pitcher, an aggressive chipper and putter and probably the greatest bunker player ever.

Next on the scene to challenge Nicklaus was a new generation. Johnny Miller, the Californian who burst to prominence with a 63 in the final round of the 1973 US Open, went on to win two dozen events including the Open at Birkdale in 1976, where he thwarted the challenge of Nicklaus and the youthful Seve Ballesteros.

Next to step up was Kansas City's Tom Watson. His five Open Championships included a thrilling tussle with Nicklaus at Turnberry in 1977, Jack shooting rounds of 66-66 on Saturday and Sunday to fall one short of Watson's 66-65. Remembered by many as the greatest Open of all time, it was capped by a putt from Jack that travelled the width of the final green, dropping in for an improbable birdie three after he'd driven into gorse bushes. But Watson had played a marvellous approach and had only a three-footer to take the title.

That spurred Watson on to more daring deeds. Earlier that year he'd won his first Masters. In the 1981 Masters, he stared down Jack again and by the end was slipping on the Green Jacket for the second time. And at the 1982 US Open at Pebble Beach, Watson holed a chip shot out of deep rough beside the 71st green, giving him the birdie he needed for victory.

But when Jack lost, he lost graciously – and he always came back. Nicklaus was winning majors before Player, Trevino, Miller and Watson came along, and he was winning them after they stopped. His last hurrah came in the 1986 Masters, when he had not won a tournament in two years.

With nine holes to go, the 46-year-old Nicklaus, five strokes off the lead, summoned nine holes of the most electrifying golf the game has seen, blitzing through the back nine in 30 strokes and roaring past his young rivals to a one-stroke victory and a record sixth Green Jacket.

Nicklaus' career is incomparable. No one has won more Masters, US Opens

ABOVE Gary Player – "The more I practise, the luckier I get."

or USPGAs, and although others have won more Open Championships, no one can match Jack's seven runner-up finishes to go with his three victories. Along with his 18 champion-ship titles, Jack finished second in the majors no fewer than 19 times.

Until Tiger Woods manages to surpass Nicklaus' major record, there is no point anyone wasting their breath in debate. Nicklaus is still the greatest.

Chapter 9

The Famous Five

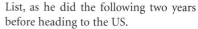

THE TWELVE MONTHS SPANNING April 1957 to March 1958 was perhaps the most significant year in the history of European golf. Five bouncing babies – Seve Ballesteros, Nick Faldo, Sandy Lyle, Bernhard Langer and Ian Woosnam – came into this world. Within a couple of decades, they had transformed the face of European golf.

Here's how the 'Famous Five' did it.

Seve Ballesteros

IT IS FITTING THAT SEVE SHOULD be the eldest of the group, for it was he, born for such a role, who led the European charge.

It is impossible to exaggerate Seve's explosive impact on the game in the late 1970s. As if his good looks and film star smile were not enough to grab attention, he played golf like his life depended on every swash-buckling swing.

At the age of just 19, in 1976, Seve almost won the Open Championship at Birkdale, just losing out to Johnny Miller. The chip-and-run shot that he threaded through bunkers on the 72nd green, to save par and tie second, was labelled "the shot that was heard around the world", and it was an emphatic statement of intent. By the end of that year, Seve had topped the European Money List, as he did the following two years before heading to the US.

By that time, he was Open

Champion, after a daredevil last round at Royal Lytham had snatched the trophy from under Hale Irwin's nose.

Seve smashed drives to every corner of the course, yet kept making pars and the occasional birdie.

ABOVE Severiano Ballesteros in the sandhills of Royal Birkdale, 1976

BELOW
Seve Ballesteros after the World Match Play tournament in 1984

BELOW
Seve Ballesteros after the World Match Play tournament in 1984

Some American journalists said he'd never win the US Masters because of his driving, but it wasn't nearly as wild as they thought. Seve was a smart thinker who knew what he was doing, and he was also a genius. He won the 1980 Masters like he was strolling in the park.

Seve's game was made for Augusta. There was more room off the tee than at most other championships, and no rough to speak of, so he could smash his driver as hard as he liked. At the time, he was one of the game's longest hitters and Augusta's slick, sloping greens placed huge emphasis on the short game skills in which Seve was king. As a boy he'd taught himself to play with a 3-iron and pebbles on the beach, so chipping for real must have seemed easy. He won his second green jacket in 1983, and everyone thought he'd go on to win more. But he never won the Masters again.

Indeed, from the age of 31, Seve did not win another major. Someone with that much talent should have got his hands on more major trophies than his total of five.

Seve was never the most consistent of golfers, even in his prime, so when his game started to go off the boil when he was in his late thirties, everyone thought, "oh, he'll soon be back". But he never has been back, not really.

Nick Faldo

NEXT INTO THIS WORLD WAS
Nick Faldo, on July 18 1957. Thirty
years later, he stood triumphant at
Muirfield celebrating his first major
victory, the Open Championship. He
quickly added two more Opens,
interspersed with three Masters wins,
and his tally of six majors is evidence of
his right to be described as Britain's
greatest golfer.

Faldo and golf didn't meet until after
his 14th birthday, but within four years
he was English Amateur champion. He
turned professional a year later, and
soon won his first pro tournament,
catapulting himself into the 1977
Ryder Cup team. This was when the
golfing world started to take notice of
Nick Faldo.

Playing with Peter Oosterhuis in the
first day fourballs and foursomes, he
won both matches, with Jack Nicklaus
and Ray Floyd among the scalps. In the
final day singles he came up against
Tom Watson, recently crowned Open
Champion, and beat him too. Still only
20, Faldo didn't mind giving the world's
best golfers a thrashing.

Faldo was a long hitter and his
elegant, upright swing produced
towering iron shots. He had a sweet

ABOVE Nick Faldo
aged 21

ball-striking reached near perfection and he seemed mentally stronger, and for six or seven years, Faldo was the dominant golfer in the world.

No one else prepared so fastidiously for championships as Nick, and once on the course he withdrew into a cocoon of concentration. This single-minded approach and seeming lack of personality left him open to potshots, and for years he endured a fractious relationship with the media. But in the late 1990s, Faldo's golf was not what it had once been, the newspapers softened up on him and we saw the softer side of Nick.

Now he can look back with satisfaction on a career record of nine victories on the PGA tour and no fewer than 34 others.

Bernhard Langer

IN THE EARLY 1970S, TEACHING guru John Jacobs was talking to a German teaching professional about a young assistant pro he had working for him. "He is the most incredible ball-striker," enthused the teaching pro, "but

ABOVE Nick Faldo holds the Claret Jug after winning the Open in 1990

short game and could putt the lights out when the mood took him. He became a winning machine – and then he decided he needed an overhaul, with David Leadbetter the mechanic.

After a couple of years in which he got to grips with his new swing, Faldo emerged better in every way. His

he's an absolutely terrible putter." The teenager's name was Bernhard Langer.

Langer was for a long time one of Europe's best ball-strikers and shot-makers, but no one has suffered more agony on the greens. Since turning pro at an age when most youngsters are still at school, Langer has had to fight a golfer's worst affliction – the yips.

It's a psychological condition with physical effects: the muscles behave as if with a will of their own, making holing putts a nightmare. Traditionally, the yips hit golfers late in their careers; the fact that Langer had to deal with them pretty much from day one, and was phenomenally successful, tells you a lot about the rest of his game.

Amazingly, though, Langer was mostly a very good putter. He won two Masters on the fastest, scariest greens in the world, and got the ball in the hole often enough to stay at the top in Europe for a long time.

To do so, he had to resort to unorthodox methods. At first, he sought solutions with a change of equipment, but soon switched from an orthodox putting stroke to a cross-handed grip, with the left hand below the right. That worked fine – he won the US Masters in

1985, holding off Seve Ballesteros. But the yips came back, so he found another method, clamping his left wrist against

BELOW Bernhard Langer – the most incredible ball-striker

BELOW
Bernhard Langer (right)
after the Masters, in
April 1985

the putter shaft, clasping his forearm with his left hand. The putts started dropping again but once more, the yips returned. So, finally, Langer went to the broomhandle putter.

Bernhard possesses an inner strength, thanks to his deeply held religious faith, hard work and determination. Most pros, given similar turmoil on the greens, would have settled for making a living from teaching. But Langer kept on playing.

If his career seems to be defined by his troubles with the "short stick", that does not do the man credit. Very few players have been able to sustain the high quality of golf that Langer did from 1972, when he turned pro. If you factor his troubles on the greens into his tally of nearly 60 wins around the world and two Masters titles, it's a spectacular achievement.

Langer commands respect and affection both sides of the fairway ropes. A man of integrity and manners, he was the model Ryder Cup captain in 2004, when he guided Europe to victory by a record margin.

Sandy Lyle

NICK FALDO BEAT SANDY LYLE into this world by five months, but when it came to golf there was a time when it seemed Lyle would pip Faldo to the post in almost everything they did.

But then he did get a head start; by the time he was 14, Lyle was hitting 600 balls a day. He played for England boys at 14 and was English Amateur champion at 17 and 19, and this effortless momentum carried on into his pro career.

This is when Lyle and Faldo started to dovetail. Sandy won the Open at Royal St George's in 1985; Nick won it at Muirfield two years later. Sandy won the US Masters in 1988 (the first Brit to do so); Nick won it a year later. The pair were at the heart of Europe's Ryder Cup renaissance when, under the leadership of Tony Jacklin, they played like the world-beaters they were.

During the mid-1980s, Sandy seemed unstoppable, with the game to win wherever he teed it up. In an era when driver clubheads were made of timber, he could launch the ball distances that would be considered long even today.

ABOVE Sandy Lyle kisses the Claret Jug after winning the 1985 Open at Royal St Georges Golf Club in Sandwich

And his prowess with a 1-iron is legendary; he was quite simply the best in the world.

Allied to that power, Sandy had a soft touch on and around the greens. And even if he did drop a shot or two, he produced so many stunning strokes that

apart. Maybe over the years the bad shots chipped away at his inner self-belief, maybe Sandy just forgot how to play well. Whatever, within three years of winning the Masters he was a shadow of his former self.

He remains a wonderful golfer to watch. The wins might have dried up, but Sandy is still the same talented, amiable bloke with the laid-back nature.

Ian Woosnam

IAN WOOSNAM IS THE BABY of Europe's Famous Five. Not that this had anything to do with him being the last to win a European Tour event. The fact is, Woosie was a late developer.

He turned pro around the same time as the rest, but while they got on with the business of winning, Woosie struggled, forced to travel in a camper van eating baked beans out of a tin.

Woosnam was born on the English side of the border, to Welsh parents. He learnt to play on a course that had 15 holes in Wales and three in England, so it's fitting that he should fly the flag for Wales.

Although not tall, Woosnam

he always gave himself birdie and eagle opportunities.

At the end of the 1980s and into the 1990s, the careers of Lyle and Faldo went their separate ways. As Faldo went from strength to strength with his new swing, Sandy's game started to fall

for the next 12 years and in 1987 won more than £1 million, becoming the first British player to win the World Matchplay. Then, in 2001, he became the first player ever to win that tournament in three different decades and, at 43, the oldest ever winner.

Woosnam's game is blessed with all the ingredients of a winner – tenacity, bottle, passion, a powerful long game and a delicate short game. He has been a great golfer to watch.

He would surely have won more than one major – the 1991 Masters – had it not been for a slight weakness with the putter. While he hasn't suffered quite as badly as Langer, it's been miserable enough, but it has never eaten away at the rest of his game. He's just kept peppering the pins.

And he hasn't done too badly: around £8 million in career prize money and 44 tournament wins. Woosie has won in style, and he's hardly likely to have many regrets.

LEFT Ian Woosnam with the green jacket after the final round of the Masters, held at The Augusta National Golf Club in April 1991

developed a strong physique, is a powerful ball-striker and has an admired swing. It seems amazing that he took so long to break through, but he had to go three times to the infamous European Tour Qualifying School, graveyard of many aspiring golf pros, before he made enough cash on the main tour to retain his card. Once he had a foothold, though, Woosnam made great strides.

He wasn't out of the money list top 11

Chapter 10

The Greatest Courses

St Andrews

THE SCOTS INVENTED GOLF, AND this is where it all started. This is the Home of Golf.

There are more than 100 holes at St Andrews on the east coast of Scotland, but the main attraction is the 'Old Course'. It's like nothing else on earth: pot bunkers, vast double greens, more bumps than a teenager's duvet and wonderfully springy turf.

You stand on the first tee staring at the widest fairway in the game and, minutes later, you're marching towards four hours of challenging, joyous golf. And the best is saved for last ... and sec-ond last: the 17th, arguably the most famous hole in the world, known as the 'Road Hole'. Making a double-bogey will never have seemed such fun. At the 18th, savour golf's most famous view as you aim your drive at the clock on the R&A clubhouse – and try to avoid hitting the old grey town on your right-hand side.

Think about who's played St Andrews – Bobby Jones, Jack Nicklaus, Arnold

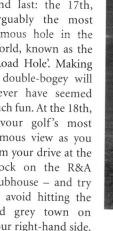

Palmer, Seve Ballesteros, Nick Faldo and Tiger Woods. And given the choice of only one golf course to play for the rest of their lives, some of these illustrious names would choose this above any other.

ABOVE Jack Nicklaus stands on the Swilcan bridge at St Andrews

Augusta National

IN THE 1930S, A GLINT CAME INTO the eye of Bobby Jones, who had decided that winning golf tournaments was a bit tedious. What better challenge than building one of the most beautiful golf courses in the world?

Jones teamed up with golf course architect Alister Mackenzie, and together they created Augusta National. And soon after the project was completed, Jones instigated an invitational tournament: The Masters.

The 11th, 12th and 13th at Augusta – the infamous loop of holes known as Amen Corner – are the most famous three holes in golf. They are also among the hardest.

The 11th features an unremarkable drive followed by an unnerving second, downhill to a kidney-shaped green guarded by water. The par-3 12th, played over water to a green a dozen or so paces deep, is the closest a pro gets to 'hit, hope and pray'. On the par-5 13th, after a 300-yard hook shot round the corner of the dogleg fairway, you're looking at a long-iron, off a sloping lie, to a green guarded by bunkers side and back, with Rae's Creek protecting the front.

To walk those carpet-like fairways and take in the fresh Georgia air, perfumed with the aroma of azaleas... could golf get any better?

Pebble Beach

PERCHED ON CALIFORNIA'S rugged Monterey Peninsula, Pebble Beach is a spectacular spot – a gentle lob-wedge from the Pacific Ocean.

And the course has played host to some of the greatest US Opens: Jack Nicklaus in 1972, Tom Watson in 1982, Tiger Woods and his 15-shot win in

2000. But anyone can play at Pebble Beach. Just as at St Andrews, you can walk this hallowed turf.

The course's par-3 7th is small but scary. Its yardage barely makes it into three figures, but the line of play takes the golfer straight towards the Pacific, and it can get breezy. Bunkers and deep rough either side of the very narrow green aren't friendly. Even the pros get twitchy on this hole.

At the par-5 18th, the first two shots flirt with the ocean front, as the fairway gently doglegs to the left. There was a time when the 550-odd yardage kept the green out of reach in two, but nowadays pros wing it on to the green with a drive and long-iron. In the real world, though, it's still a fearsome finishing hole.

But don't think Pebble Beach is a two-hole wonder: it more than lives up to the hype.

BELOW
The spectacular setting of the Pebble Beach Golf Course

Cypress Point

NEXT DOOR TO PEBBLE BEACH lies Cypress Point – and it's no poor relation. In the golf magazine rankings, Pebble wins pretty much every time, but Cypress Point has its own charms and it's hard not to fall for them.

For starters, you've got the same gorgeous location. You've also got a fantastic golf course, designed by Dr Alister Mackenzie. The fairways meander through avenues of huge Monterey cypress trees, leading to heavily contoured greens where sculpted bunkers lie in wait.

If you're a big hitter, the front nine could be your happy hunting ground because it contains four par-5s and a couple of cracking par-3s. It's not monstrously long, either.

On the back nine there's no let-up in the entertainment stakes, for the emphasis is on shot-making. The par-3 16th is well over 200 yards, all of which requires an airborne carriage over the Pacific Ocean. It's a similar scenario on the intimidating but spectacular 17th. Slice your drive and you'll miss not just the fairway, but terra firma altogether.

No one ever came away from Cypress Point anything other than invigorated by one of the most enthralling experiences the world of golf has to offer.

Royal County Down

WHEN TOM WATSON first played this course, he said it included the finest consecutive 11 holes of links golf in the world. The other seven aren't shabby, either.

Book yourself a flight to Northern Ireland and a tee time, preferably when the yellow gorse is in bloom. You'll probably want to walk straight from the 18th green on to the first tee to do it all again.

If you don't fall in love with the front nine at Royal County Down, you surely aren't a golfer. In the mighty shadow of the purple and blue mountains of Mourne, the course follows the rugged curve of Dundrum Bay. You'll be captivated by the challenge that unfolds in front of you, described by Herbert Warren Wind as the sternest of any he'd experienced.

But you'll get a stiff neck from looking over your shoulder at the stunning views.

Happily, the short 4th hole turns you to face the mountains for the first time.

BELOW
The spectacular view of the 14th hole at the Royal County Down Club

From there on there's no respite for the golfing senses, as verdant green fairways weave through golden swathes of gorse either side.

It can be uncompromisingly difficult, but this is one kind of punishment you could never get enough of.

Royal
Melbourne

THERE ARE PLENTY OF PLACES with greater concentrations of golf courses than Melbourne. But few cities can boast such a cluster of top-quality layouts – and the best among them is the 36 holes to be found at Royal Melbourne.

The landscape is not dissimilar to that of a Scottish links, rugged and with an abundance of heather and bracken, and Scotsman Dr Alister Mackenzie had a hand in its creation, along with Australian Open champion Alex Russell. Their success can be judged by the fact that it is the best golf course in Australia and one of the best in the world.

Ernie Els says it's one of his favourite courses, and he believes Royal Melbourne has the best greens in the world. But there are other reasons to make a pilgrimage to Australia: it's a classic all-round test of golf.

The rugged bunkers represent avoid-at-all-costs hazards. The undulations of the fairways and greens take advantage of the rolling landscape, and it's a real shot-maker's course. The 18th is a simply magnificent par-4.

Royal Melbourne has a reputation as a stern test of golf, but that doesn't detract from the pleasure it gives golfers of all standards. This is world-class golf for the masses.

Turnberry

THE AILSA COURSE AT TURNBERRY nearly became a casualty of the Second World War. The old course, dug up to build an RAF airfield, nearly remained buried under concrete after the war.

But it was rescued by architect Mackenzie Ross, and it was worth saving. It has a jaw-dropper of a location on the west coast of Scotland, offering views across the Mull of Kintyre to the Isle of Arran. To the south-west, only Ailsa Craig, a giant Christmas pudding-shaped rock, interrupts the view.

But it took a single weekend of golf to put Turnberry truly on the map. In the 1977 Open, Tom Watson and Jack Nicklaus were locked in perhaps the greatest championship of all time. By the weekend, they had left the field trailing; they then battled head-to-head with shots of inspiration and brilliance. Only a single shot separated them at the end.

At Turnberry, you don't necessarily have to be a long driver, but you do have to be straight. This keeps you shy of wiry grasses and dunes, and enables you to fire iron shots from the crisp turf and seek out the flags, usually tucked behind bunkers.

It is an awe-inspiring test of golf.

BELOW Pine Valley Golf Club

Pine Valley

BUSINESSMAN GEORGE CRUMP, a mad-keen golfer, had been looking for years for the perfect plot of land on which to build a course. Then he spotted Pine Valley – 200 acres of New Jersey forest and marshland –

BELOW The 17th hole at the Valderrama Golf Club

while looking out of a train window.

This isn't your typical golf course. The fairways are laid out like green carpets between vast expanses of trees, undergrowth, water and sandy scrubland. Nowhere could the consequences of missing a fairway be more apparent. You know that if you hit it solidly off the tee, you may stand a chance of playing to your handicap. If you miss too many fairways, it's goodnight.

The greens are designed and protected in similar fashion, with cunning run-offs punishing slightly stray approach shots. Anything a little more

wayward finds serious trouble. One of the greenside bunkers is called 'The Devil's Arse', which says it all.

Pine Valley members offer a standing bet to all first-time visitors, challenging them to break 80. Those members are a pretty shrewd bunch.

Valderrama

WHEN BILLIONAIRE JAIME ORTEZ Patino decided he wanted to build the Augusta National of Europe, he got in touch with golf course architect Robert Trent Jones and together they transformed an unremarkable layout in the south of Spain into continental Europe's finest golf course.

Valderrama is a fine championship test from the back tees and a very playable course from the more forward tees, so golfers of all standards can appreciate its charms.

The greens' grass is so fine that the putting surfaces are billiard-table smooth. The attention to detail is quite staggering and it makes the whole playing experience easy on the eye.

let's dwell on the names of the golfers who have won an Open Championship at Muirfield. Introducing Walter Hagen, Henry Cotton, Gary Player, Jack Nicklaus, Lee Trevino, Tom Watson and Nick Faldo... what more do you need to know?

Muirfield is one of the world's purest, fairest, stiffest, classic tests of links golf. Old Tom Morris, who originally penned the layout, and Harry Colt, who tweaked it into its current form, produced a masterpiece.

What you see is what you get. When you stand on the tee, everything is there in front of you: the ideal line, the hazards, all the information you need to pick the right shot. When you're staring at the green, it's the same story.

But Muirfield is a shot-maker's heaven on earth. The humps, hollows and undulations of the fairways and greens are made for golf. The 160 or so bunkers is an unusually high number, but at least you can see where they are.

Good shots get rewarded and bad shots get punished, although the capriciousness of the bounce can produce good or bad breaks. But if you're playing at Muirfield, it's your lucky day.

And technically speaking, it's a fine layout. There is a selection of holes that dogleg both ways, but the fairways aren't so narrow as to make the course unplayable to the average golfer. Instead, the main challenge lies in the second shots.

Cork trees tiptoe on to the fairway and partially block the line to the flag. Greenside bunkering represents an aesthetically pleasing form of added protection.

Whatever the numbers at the bottom of the scorecard, a round at Valderrama is something to savour.

Muirfield

AN ACCURATE BAROMETER OF A golf course's credentials is its roll call of championship winners. So

Chapter 11

21st Century Golf

A HUNDRED YEARS DOESN'T seem that long, but when you see that the game of golf in this period is bookended by the contrasting images of Harry Vardon and Tiger Woods, it suddenly seems an awfully long time. It barely seems the same game.

What would Vardon, James Braid and JH Taylor, who dominated golf around the start of the 20th century, make of the game today? We could put them on, say, Augusta National, persuade Tiger Woods to make up a fourball and have him tee off first, so he could launch one of his drives 350 yards.

We'd kit out the old timers in long trousers – none of those silly plus-fours – and a soft cotton shirt instead of a starchy collar and tie. We'd swap their hickory-shafts for graphite, their crude clubheads for high-tech perimeter-weighted models with super grippy grooves, their wooden-headed drivers for titanium, and their primitive balls for high-spinning, long-distance, rubber bullets. By then they'd scarcely recognise the game, although they might enjoy the extra 100-yard walk from the tee to their ball.

Mind you, they're not used to 7,000-yard golf courses. It was more like 6,000 in their day. Still, we could arrange for an electric trolley… no, you can never beat a good old-fashioned caddie.

But is golf going to change as much in the next 100 years as it has in the last 100? Perhaps the more pressing question is: do we want it to change as much?

Golf's doing fine at the moment. We are in the era of the Tiger, who may be on his way to becoming the greatest player ever, but before he came along, South African Ernie Els was touted as the man most likely to dominate.

He won a hat-trick of South African titles – the Masters, PGA and Open – in one season, an achievement that prompted Gary Player to say, "When I first saw Ernie play golf I knew I was witnessing one of golf's next generation of superstars." Soon after joining the European Tour, he travelled to Dubai for the Desert Classic and tore the Emirates course apart, shooting a first round 61, 11-under par, that is regarded as one of the tour's greatest rounds.

Ernie then embarked on a global smash and grab of golf's trophy cabinet. In 1994, he won his first US Open at Oakmont, with a display of powerful hitting and assured holing-out. That year he won three separate world titles.

In 1997 he won his second US Open at the uncompromising Congressional Country Club.

LEFT Ernie Els during a practice round for the 2006 HSBC World Matchplay Championship at Wentworth

BELOW Ernie Els raises
his arms after winning
the 1997 US Open
Championship

When the moment of truth arrived, on the par-4 17th, he struck a nerveless 5-iron that homed in on a pin placed perilously close to water: probably the shot of the year.

Els endured a few near misses between those two US Open wins, but he was gathering trophies fast and it was no big surprise when he triumphed in the 2002 Open Championship in a playoff.

That week at Muirfield, all the best things about Ernie's game were in evidence. His second round 66 was a display of effortless power and precision. His final round stumble on the par-3 16th revealed a fallible side, but he shrugged it off by birdying the next hole and emerging triumphant from the playoff.

Later that year, Els played one of the most astonishing rounds in the history of the World Matchplay Championship, a 12-under-par 60 that lit up Wentworth's West Course. He then propelled his huge frame to new heights. At the start of 2003 he averaged 65 over the four rounds of the Mercedes Championship, smashing the US Tour scoring record with his 31-under par aggregate. By the end of the year, he'd won seven times and bagged the top spot on Europe's Order of

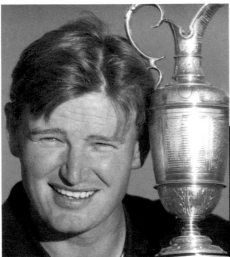

He won three straight US Junior Amateur Championships, then three straight US Amateur Championships. Not even Bobby Jones could hold a candle to that kind of record.

In his first major championship as a professional, the 1997

LEFT Ernie Els with the Claret Jug after winning the 131st Open Championship at Muirfield, 2002

BELOW Tiger Woods with the trophy after his two-stroke victory at the Deutsche Bank Championship, 2006

Merit. In 2004 he played surely the round of the year: a 12-under-par 60 at Royal Melbourne, a score that many thought impossible.

As defending champion of the Dubai Desert Classic in 2006, Ernie came up against a certain T Woods Esq in a one-hole playoff ... and lost.

That Tiger should become the best player on the planet was no surprise; everyone saw him coming. His dad said Tiger had switched to an interlocking grip when he was still in nappies.

US Masters, records fell like ninepins. Having played the front nine in a disappointing 40, he blitzed the back nine in 30 to finish with a two-under-par 70, then shot 66, 65 on Friday and Saturday. On Sunday, he cruised to a closing 69.

By the end of the week, Tiger was wearing a green jacket and he'd beaten Jack Nicklaus' lowest ever 72-hole total (270); set the largest 54-hole lead (nine shots); the largest winning margin (12 shots); the most shots under par for the back nine (-16); the most threes in one week (26) ... oh, and he was the youngest ever winner (21 years, three months and 14 days).

More remarkable even than that performance, Tiger won the centenary US Open at Pebble Beach in 2000 by 15 shots. In a week where no other golfer managed to finish under par, he was 12-under. That same year he won the Open Championship at St Andrews by eight shots, becoming only the fifth man to win all four of golf's major championships.

But even that Open win paled into

insignificance when soon afterwards Tiger was in possession of all four major trophies at the same time. Technically, it wasn't a Grand Slam: it wasn't in the same calendar year. But in every other respect it was a Grand Slam, and it was nothing short of spectacular.

In 2003 and 2004, Tiger at least proved he's human. He continued to win tournaments on the PGA Tour, but he didn't win majors. By 2005, however, the Tiger was roaring again, racking up wins in the Masters and the Open Championship, and the following year saw him collecting his third Open victory and dominating the field to take the USPGA again.

Tiger's eyes, and those of the entire golf world, are on Jack Nicklaus's record of 18 professional major victories. For him to surpass that landmark is a tall order, but at the time of writing he can boast 12 major wins – all collected before he'd turned 30.

Can anyone stop Tiger in his tracks? No. But check his stride from time to time and win more than just the occasional major? Phil Mickelson and Vijay Singh are two possibilities.

Vijay – fittingly, his name is Hindi for 'victory' – is a hard worker with an almost effortless golf swing. He's also a model of consistency, able to register top-10 finishes with uncanny regularity.

The Fijian, who turned pro in 1982 but had to wait until 1998 for his first major – the USPGA – has since added a Masters title and another USPGA. But golf lovers everywhere will always remember Vijay for his stunning exploits in 2004, when he won a massive nine times, achieved 18 top-10 finishes and led the PGA Tour money list.

He didn't have it all his own way

BELOW Tiger Woods (left) shakes hands with Vijay Singh

that year. Left-hander Phil Mickelson became a major winner by taking the 2004 Masters in spectacular fashion, in the most exciting Masters since Jack Nicklaus took the title in 1986.

Phil put up an incredible back-nine performance on that memorable Sunday, pipping Ernie Els with a last-hole birdie-three. It gave him the confidence he needed to challenge anew for golf's top honours, and he duly won the Masters again in 2006, a year after he'd come away from Baltusrol with the USPGA title.

Then there's the new breed of young guns. The roll call of aspiring megastars includes Sergio Garcia, Luke Donald, Adam Scott, Paul Casey and Trevor Immelman, to name just five. There are many others aiming to make their names in the glamorous world of top-level pro golf.

So we can safely say the game is in good hands. But is the equipment in the hands of the top players damaging the game?

Recent years have seen rapid developments in the way clubs are built, the materials used and the way they perform. The rules of golf control the dimensions and make-up of clubs, and the Royal and Ancient and the United States Golf Association watch developments keenly to ensure innovations conform. But shafts have got longer and

LEFT The putter and golf balls of Phil Mickelson

BELOW Phil Mickelson's golf bag containing two drivers

lighter, clubheads have grown bigger and the properties of the materials used mean the ball comes off the clubface hotter and faster.

Miss-hits are no longer punished in the same way as 30 years ago. A 'necky' strike with a persimmon driver would see the ball take off low and slice weakly to the right. The same strike with an enormous titanium-headed driver produces a shot that is almost indistinguishable from a pure hit.

Golf ball technology has accelerated even faster. In real terms, the ball is responsible for probably an extra 30 or 40 yards in the average drive of the leading tour pros over the last decade or so.

It is argued by some that technology is in danger of ruining the game, and it has massive implications for the way golf courses are designed, for fairway bunkers are being made redundant as pros drive straight over them.

It's becoming normal for par-5s to be reduced to a driver and mid-iron approach shot. Par-4s are frequently overpowered with a driver, sand-wedge approach, and often a driver isn't needed: a long-iron tee shot and mid-iron second are enough. As a result, classic layouts such as Sunningdale Old Course are considered too easy and too short to host a pro tournament.

ABOVE Golf Clubs – is the way they're produced ruining the game?

the R&A and the USGA test it to ensure it conforms to the rules. Recent years have seen moves to limit the 'spring-like' effect of clubs and the updating of distance standards for balls.

But perhaps golf course design now needs to turn in two directions to satisfy the needs of both the amateur and professional game. You won't get too many average players queuing up to play 8,000-yard courses.

While golf club technology has been going crazy, however, club golfers' average handicap has remained static. The equipment gets better, but we don't. To the average golfer, the improvement in equipment manifests itself in harmless, albeit pleasing, results.

Golf balls are more durable so don't need replacing as often – but they're just as easy to lose as they always were. Tour pros might be spinning balls back on the greens as if tugged on a piece of string, but the typical amateur is happy for the ball simply to stop somewhere on the green. Modern drivers make the ball go a bit further, especially on miss-hits, but certainly nowhere near as

Increasing yardages are now golf courses' main form of defence. The 2006 Masters, for example, was played over 7,445 yards, having been extended from 7,290 yards with the lengthening of six of Augusta National's holes.

The race to produce innovative equipment is continuing, even though

dramatically as in the pro game. Generally speaking, the benefits to amateurs are psychological.

So maybe we have nothing to worry about. Concerns over equipment technology are probably only relevant to the top 0.1 per cent of the golfing population. Joe Soap is not going to stop playing classic golf courses because they're no longer much of a challenge.

For the 99.9 per cent of people who play golf for fun, the game doesn't look set to change nearly as much in the next century as it did in the last. Even if the equipment looks different, the essence of the game will remain the same. It will always be engaging, entertaining, uplifting, challenging and at times infuriating.

None of us would have it any other way.

BELOW The par 4, 17th hole (foreground) with the par 4, 18th hole and clubhouse behind on the Old Course at Sunningdale Golf Club, June 2005

Chapter 12

Ryder Cup
Dream Teams

The European Dream Team, selected by Bernard Gallacher, 1995 Ryder Cup winning captain

Nick Faldo

Nick Faldo could genuinely intimidate opponents. Just the appearance of his name on a leaderboard was enough to make people jump, and then there was the sheer physical, 6ft 4in and 15 stone presence of the man.

And Faldo has played more Ryder Cup matches, and won more points, than any other golfer. In moments of intense pressure, he came up with the goods.

In the 1995 Ryder Cup at Oak Hill, playing the 18th against Curtis Strange,

Faldo was 100 yards from the pin and needing to get down in two to win the Ryder Cup. And he did exactly that, pitching to 4ft and holing the putt. Under pressure, he was the man, and Faldo's game was relentless in its brilliance.

Seve Ballesteros

That Seve should strike what Jack Nicklaus called "one of the greatest shots I've ever seen," sums up his influence on the Ryder Cup. Seve helped transform the encounters from one-sided thrashings into well-matched contests.

The shot Nicklaus was talking about, against Tom Kite in 1983 at Palm Beach,

on others. When Jose Maria Olazabal first played in 1987, the pair of them began one of the greatest partnerships in the history of the competition.

was a 3-wood from a fairway bunker on to the final green. It only got him half a point, but it was half a point more than anyone else would have got.

Seve was the most exciting, charismatic golfer ever to grace the Ryder Cup, and his brilliance rubbed off

Brian Barnes

Brian Barnes was a natural golfing talent who may not have fulfilled his potential. But he won his share of tournaments (10) and is known as the man who beat Jack Nicklaus twice in one day.

It was at Laurel Valley in 1975, when there were two singles matches in a day. In the morning, Barnes went out and thrashed the best player in the world 4 & 2. At lunchtime, Nicklaus said, "he's beaten me once, but he won't beat me again". But Barnes went out and gave him another hiding, this time by 2 & 1.

Great Britain & Ireland lost

that Ryder Cup quite heavily. On the plane home, though, perhaps Barnes afforded himself a little smile of satisfaction.

Neil Coles

On paper, Neil Coles' Ryder Cup record might not look sensational, but his time coincided with a period of US domination. Between 1961 and 1977, when Coles was a member of the GB&I team, the US won seven encounters and lost none. But in that time he compiled a highly respectable record, playing in 40 matches and being unbeaten in 19 of them.

Coles was a class act. His swing had a metronomic rhythm, whichever club he had in his hands. He caressed the golf ball with sweet timing and good technique and was one of the great fairway wood players.

If it hadn't been for a terrible fear of flying, Coles would have been far more famous, successful and wealthy than he became.

Tony Jacklin

Think of Tony Jacklin and the Ryder Cup and two images spring to mind:

Jack Nicklaus conceding him a 30in putt at Birkdale in 1969 that meant the cup was tied, and a smiling Captain Fantastic, leading Europe to victories at the Belfry in 1985 and Muirfield Village in 1987.

Jacklin deserves all the credit he gets

for helping transform Europe into a team of world-beaters. It's a shame his playing performances aren't given more credence.

For a while the best golfer in the world, he was the linchpin of the GB&I team for seven consecutive cups and in 35 matches he was unbeaten 21 times.

Jacklin as a player was awesome, as a captain even more so. That will probably be his enduring legacy.

Colin Montgomerie

Monty's Ryder Cup debut was a baptism of fire. At Kiawah Island in

LEFT Neil Coles sinks a putt

BELOW European team Captain Tony Jacklin poses with the trophy after the Ryder Cup at The Belfry in 1985

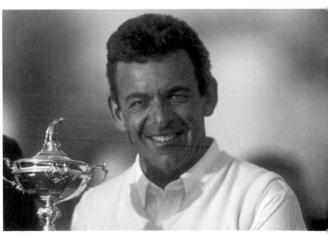

1991 – the notorious 'War on the Shore' – he was thrust into the foursomes, alongside mild-mannered David Gilford, against one of America's 'tough nut' pairings – Lanny Wadkins and Hale Irwin.

They went down 4&2, but Monty was able to steady himself and come back to win a fourball, and then gain a fighting half against Mark Calcavecchia. Although the Cup was lost, Monty could hold his head high.

At the Belfry in 1993, he played like the European No 1 he was about to become. The Ryder Cup seems to bring out the best in Monty, as in the 2002 contest, when he led the victorious Europeans from the front.

Sergio Garcia

The Spaniard could scarcely have made a more sensational Ryder Cup debut. Wearing European colours for the first time at Brookline in 1999, Garcia was in the morning foursomes on the first day, partnered with Jesper Parnevik against none other than Tiger Woods and Tom Lehman. Garcia and the Swede were magnificent, winning 2 & 1.

The pair went out in the afternoon and beat Phil Mickelson and Jim Furyk, then beat Payne Stewart and Justin Leonard the following morning. Three games, three wins.

Garcia lives and breathes the Ryder Cup, so motivation is not a problem for him. And he's a great matchplayer, as we saw at the 2002, 2004 and 2006 Ryder Cups, when he formed a magical partnership with Lee Westwood.

Bernhard Langer

The German was the perfect playing partner – solid, dependable, made very few unforced errors, and always held his nerve. Add the fact that Langer captained the Europeans to a record victory in 2004 – $18\frac{1}{2}$ points to $9\frac{1}{2}$ – and you have a Ryder Cup legend.

Langer chose a tough year for his first Ryder Cup, for at Walton Heath in 1981 the US assembled its greatest ever team. But around that time the Europeans got the hang of winning, and Langer played a critical role.

In the seven Ryder Cups after his debut, he won many more matches than he lost. It would have been fitting had he holed that infamous putt on

the final green against Hale Irwin at Kiawah Island.

ABOVE Bernhard Langer poses with the Ryder Cup

Jose Maria Olazabal

With Seve Ballesteros, Ollie formed arguably the most successful partnership in Ryder Cup history. Thrust into battle with his inspirational countryman at Muirfield Village in 1987, he thrived on the pressure, at times appearing the stronger of the two.

His sensational performance helped Europe to their first victory on US soil. Ollie's jig of delight on the 18th green is one of the Cup's enduring images.

He was possibly on his way to

Oosty won his last pro tournament at just 33, the same year he played in his swansong Ryder Cup. By then he had a better-than-50 per cent record from 28 matches, a fine effort during a lean period for the GB&I team. It's a shame that he wasn't able to be a part of the European glory years.

compiling one of the Cup's most impressive records, but a foot injury sidelined him for two years. When he returned for the 1997 matches in Valderrama, he played a pivotal part in Europe's win. This time Seve was his captain, not his playing partner. But the dynamic duo had struck again.

Peter Oosterhuis

Until Monty won seven straight Order of Merit titles, Peter Oosterhuis held one of the most impressive records in European golf, and between 1971 and 1974 he was Europe's 'numero uno'.

Oosty was a fine player from a young age and was a seasoned campaigner by the time he partnered Nick Faldo on his debut in 1977. The pairing won both their matches on day one.

Christy O'Connor Snr

The Irishman is a colourful character, but not even his personality could outshine his golf skills. One of Christy's favourite tricks was to stand on the tee of a medium-length par-3 and hit a ball on to the green with every club in his bag.

Ian Woosnam

When Ian Woosnam played in his first Ryder Cup match, the 1983 encounter at PGA National, he told partner Sam Torrance on the first tee that he felt so nervous he was going to be sick! But Woosie came out fighting and started his round birdie, par, birdie. That was typical of the man – a class player, a fine competitor, a man with serious bottle.

Woosie played in the next seven Ryder Cups and was one of Europe's true stars. He was involved in 31 games, won 14 and halved five – and take into account the fact that in eight attempts Woosie never won a singles match.

He makes it into the European dream team because of his exploits in fourballs and foursomes.

But it wasn't until he was in his mid-20s that he started to make an impact. In 1955, when he was about to hit 30, he first stepped into the breach on Ryder Cup duty. He was still playing when the cup went to Muirfield in 1973, when he was just coming up to his 50th birthday.

Talent like his doesn't go away overnight and even in the late 1990s, he was beating his age in professional senior championships.

LEFT Christy O'Connor competes in the 1965 Ryder Cup at Royal Birkdale

BELOW Ian Woosnam poses with the Ryder Cup

The United States Dream Team, selected by George Peper

Arnold Palmer

Who else could lead the US dream team? No other American has won more matches, and no one did it quite like Arnie. His golf game was an unparalleled cocktail of skill, brute force and bravado.

Built like a middleweight boxer, Arnie was not a fan of subtlety. His crushing drives and mighty iron shots were allied to one of the best chip-and-putt short games ever seen, and when he was on his game opponents were knocked over like ninepins. His Ryder Cup record of 22 wins in 32 matches is justifiably impressive.

As Lee Trevino once said, Palmer could attract a bigger gallery to watch him tie his shoelaces than most other golfers could muster with their best efforts on the course.

Jack Nicklaus

The way he dominated the tournament scene, you'd think Jack Nicklaus would have been invincible in a head-to-head confrontation. No one knew better how to bully an opponent psychologically than he.

But Jack suffered, if you can call it that, in his Ryder Cup career. Anyone who makes a Cup team can play a bit, and they might not have beaten Jack over four rounds. But in one round, anything can happen, and on eight occasions the Golden Bear got whupped.

But Jack travelled well and he wasn't fussy about which format he chose to win at. He played 28 matches and won 17, with another three halved. For anyone else, that would be a great record. Because it's Jack, we're surprised it's not better.

Billy Casper

Few golfers can claim to have played in eight consecutive Ryder Cups. That

the end. Arnie was the weaker of the two for the experience and lost the playoff.

Casper went on to win a US Masters – in a playoff. Evidently, head-to-head was his forte.

Lee Trevino

For years, Lee Trevino worked at a driving range, collecting balls for a meagre income which he supplemented by playing money matches against all

LEFT Portrait of Jack Nicklaus taken in 2005

BELOW Billy Casper, who won the 1966 US Open, lining up a putt

Billy Casper managed this, compiling an impressive playing record, explains what kind of golfer he was. He teed it up in 37 matches and in 27 of those he was unbeaten.

Casper is best known for nailing Arnold Palmer in the 1966 US Open. Eight shots behind Arnie with only the back nine to play in the final round, Casper reeled him in like a giant fish on the end of a line, and the two were tied at

comers. He famously said that real pressure was playing for 20 bucks when you only had 10 in your back pocket.

So Trevino was a rather useful matchplayer. Those money matches taught him all he needed to know about finishing an opponent off – but always with a smile and a one-liner.

Trevino's six Ryder Cup appearances involved 30 matches and in 23 of those he was not beaten: one of the best Cup records.

He was one of the most gifted ball-strikers of his generation and, considering who was around at the time, that is saying something.

Sam Snead

Many say Sam Snead was the greatest natural talent who ever played golf. Certainly his was the most enduring talent of all. At a time when most people are looking forward to collecting their bus pass, Snead was still competing with the world's best golfers.

In matchplay, Slammin' Sam was awesome. His effortless long driving and classy iron play overwhelmed opponents and golf courses. It's just as well for the rest of the world's golfers that his putting wasn't red-hot.

Not surprisingly, in the Ryder Cup he was pretty impressive. He played 13 matches and lost only two. Imagine what the GB&I players were thinking when they stood on the first tee and saw Snead. You'd hazard a guess that they weren't overly optimistic.

ABOVE Lee Trevino smiles after missing a birdie on the eighth hole during the first day of the US Senior Open golf tournament in 2004

RIGHT Sam Snead outside the clubhouse at St Andrews, during the 1946 British Open, which he won

Lanny Wadkins

For the best part of two decades, Lanny Wadkins was a stalwart of the US Ryder Cup team. With his heart on one sleeve and the Stars and Stripes on the other, he played as though his life depended on it.

That he had bottle was never more evident than during the final-day singles at the 1983 Ryder Cup in Palm Beach. The US team was staring at home defeat, for the first time, when up stepped Wadkins. His wedge shot into the final green, which finished stone dead, was one of the greatest shots in Ryder Cup history.

He was unbeaten in 22 of his 33 matches. The 11 who took Wadkins' scalp can claim to have beaten one of the toughest matchplayers ever.

Julius Boros

Julius Boros had a swing that was smoother than honey. It didn't just look the part, though; it got the job done.

Not only was his game good enough to secure three major championships in an era that featured the likes of Jack Nicklaus and Arnold Palmer at the height of their powers, but to this day he remains the oldest person to have won a major. He clinched the 1968 USPGA Championship at the age of 48 years and four-and-a-bit months.

His game lost none of its potency in matchplay. In four Ryder Cups, Julius played 16 matches and lost only three. And keep in mind he was the grand old age of 47 when he played in his last Ryder Cup.

Larry Nelson

Serving in the Vietnam War probably put things in perspective. Larry Nelson did his time in that horrific conflict and after that, maybe a game of golf did not seem so important. Perhaps that's why he seemed impervious to pressure. Even in the biggest tournaments, he was able to keep playing his quietly efficient, methodical game.

Nelson's purple patch lasted less than a decade, but in that time he won a couple of

LEFT Lanny Wadkins holds the Ryder Cup trophy

BELOW Julius Boros, a member of the US Ryder Cup team, drives off from the 1st at Royal Birkdale, October 1965

USPGA Championships and a US Open. He also made an impression on the Ryder Cup: played 13, won nine and halved one.

Nelson didn't so much overpower a golf course as chip away at its defences. Opponents felt themselves subjected to similar treatment and, all too often, the experience proved painful.

the 'show'. In fact, the man was virtually unbeatable in head-to-head competition. In the 1920s, when the USPGA was a matchplay event, he won it four times in a row, five times in all.

In his day, there weren't so many matches in the Ryder Cup as there are now, so in the five times he played he only had nine games. He won seven of them, though, and halved another.

Hagen was great in the true sense. Whether he was winning (frequently) or losing (rarely), his attitude did not change one iota.

Hale Irwin

He looked like a bank clerk, but he got his hands on a lot more money. Before he ditched his glasses and started dominating the US Seniors Tour, Hale Irwin was one of the fiercest matchplay competitors you could ever run into.

His game wasn't flashy, he didn't have a flamboyant swing, nor did he hit the ball out of sight. But he drove the ball uncannily straight, kept his rhythm, hit

ABOVE Larry Nelson hits a putt during the second round of the Senior PGA Championship, May 2005

RIGHT Walter Hagen drives during the Open Golf Championships at Hoylake, June 1924

Walter Hagen

Golf's ultimate showman wasn't averse to a bit of gamesmanship, like walking on to the first tee and saying: "Who's going to finish second, then?" But Hagen had the 'go' to go with

a lot of greens in regulation, putted nicely and was able to stay calm under pressure.

Irwin compiled an impressive Ryder Cup record between 1975 and 1981. He then came back to Kiawah Island at the age of 46, won two matches and gained the vital half-point on the last green against Bernhard Langer.

Tom Kite

Winning majors might have been a problem for Tom Kite, but winning at matchplay definitely was not. The man was a ruthless slayer of European golfers.

In 1989 at the Belfry, he inflicted on Howard Clarke one of the heaviest defeats in Ryder Cup history – 8&7 – and in 1993 he annihilated Bernhard Langer by 5&3.

Not a long hitter, Kite used tee shots to get the ball somewhere near his 'patch' – inside 100 yards. With a wedge in his hands he was deadly,

and he could putt a bit, too.

The worst thing for the Europeans who went up against him was that the mental frailties that seemed to blight him in the major championships didn't seem to be a factor in matchplay.

Tiger Woods

Tiger's first few Ryder Cups were unspectacular affairs, during which he lost more than he won. But he was just getting into his stride.

If ever he stood a chance of getting turned over, this is the format to do it. Ryder Cup matches are only 18 holes, like a mad sprint for the finishing line. Anything can happen.

But Tiger will probably be playing Ryder Cup golf until at least 2016, by which time he'll have played in 10 of these things. Would you seriously bet that he won't be the leading points scorer of all time?

Who would win? The US dream team gets the nod by virtue of superior firepower. But we reckon it would be close. Call the scoreline 15-13.

Ryder Cup 2006

THE HISTORY OF THE great game of golf has had more than its share of emotional moments, but surely none can have been quite so intense as the time on Sunday, September 24, 2006 when Europe clinched the 36th Ryder Cup.

It all happened so quickly, within the space of a few minutes. First, Europe's Luke Donald ensured his team would retain the trophy with a five-foot putt at the 17th to beat Chad Campbell 2&1. Then rookie Swede Henrik Stenson rolled in a seven-footer at the 15th to halve the hole and take his match against Vaughn Taylor 4&3.

So the Ryder Cup was staying in

Europe. But all eyes at the K Club in Co Kildare, Ireland were on happenings at the 16th, where the man everyone wanted to win was coming towards the end of his match against Zach Johnson.

That man was Northern Ireland's Darren Clarke, a man whose presence in

BELOW A tearful Darren Clarke (left) celebrates with captain Ian Woosnam

the Europe team had been in doubt until not long before the contest got under way. His beloved wife Heather had lost her battle against breast cancer a mere six weeks before and the golf world, while grieving for Darren, had wondered whether it was right for him to be plunged into the cauldron of pressure that is the Ryder Cup.

Television viewers the world over, and the thousands gathered around the K Club's 16th green, held their breath. Moments before, just as Stenson was celebrating his victory, Clarke had played his approach shot to the green with the safety cushion of a three-hole lead. His putt failed to seal the match, but Johnson, having seen his putt stay above ground too, generously lifted Clarke's marker to concede the hole. The big man had won 3&2.

The scenes that followed will never be forgotten by anyone who witnessed them. Clarke dissolved into tears as he was embraced by Europe's team captain, Ian Woosnam, by American captain Tom Lehman, by

the world's best golfer, Tiger Woods, and by many, many others.

Amid the uncontained emotion, the celebrations began and the champagne began to flow, even though four singles matches were still to be resolved. It didn't really matter. Europe had annihilated

the US team, and the man everyone wanted to succeed had done so.

Once he had regained a little composure, Clarke told reporters that there were too many memories from the three days of Ryder Cup battle for him to recall. "But my team have been

ABOVE Darren Clarke (left) is hugged by a sympathetic Tiger Woods after winning his singles match against Zach Johnson

RIGHT
Europe's Darren Clarke
(right) is congratulated
by Zach Johnson. Cue
emotional scenes at the
K Club

unbelievable all week, so have the American guys, their wives and the crowd – their support has been incredible."

Those scenes of naked emotion provided an extraordinary and fitting climax to a quite breath-taking performance by the European team. Only a very foolish betting man – or an incredibly wise one – would have put money on the Europeans duplicating the record margin of victory they had registered two years before at Oakland Hills in Michigan. Looking again at that score (Europe 18.5, USA 9.5) hammers home the true scale of the victory – and Europe had done it twice in succession.

And they had done it in the most emphatic style imaginable, dominating every single session of play and demonstrating a remarkable team spirit. The European players were playing for each other, for the team and for big Darren, and the household-name Americans were simply shoved out of the way, despite some excellent individual performances.

No one had predicted another 18.5 – 9.5 score, and many an observer had expected the USA to claim revenge for the Oakland Hills rout. The run-up to the 2006 Cup was marked by claims

the one and only Arnold Palmer, and wouldn't it suit the US team down to the ground? If you're going to play the thing in Ireland – and why shouldn't you? – why not choose one of the country's testing links courses?

It might have suited the Americans, but as it turned out, it suited the Europeans a whole lot more.

The choice of the doughty if diminutive Woosnam as Europe's team captain had come in for some sniping, too. Was he made of the right stuff to be a leader of men? Was his wild card selection of the bereaved Clarke, ahead of the likes of Denmark's Thomas Bjorn, indicative of a man who would cope with the immense pressure of the event?

In fact, Woosnam's leadership, team selection and motivation of his crew were spot on, and although he was a mightily relieved man at the end of it

by some observers that Europe had made too many pre-tournament mistakes for the team to have a chance.

There were those in Europe who had questioned the choice of the K Club for the venue of the 36th version Ryder Cup. The K Club's Palmer Course was a glorious layout, they conceded, but hadn't it been designed by an American,

BELOW America's Tiger Woods (left) and Jim Furyk plot their next move

all, he showed no sign of buckling beneath the burden of captaincy during the three days of play.

And those three days started brightly, despite a loss in the opening fourball, for Team Europe – a team that gracious US captain Lehman later called the best the continent had ever put together.

The lovely K Club was looking at its best, bathing in sunshine after some trying, rain-affected practice sessions, as the first fourball – Europe's Padraig Harrington and Colin Montgomerie against the formidable American pairing of Tiger Woods and Jim Furyk – teed off.

Irishman Harrington was enjoying home advantage, but he and Monty soon found themselves three holes down as Woods and Furyk found early form and birdies aplenty from the eighth hole onwards. The Europeans fought back to reduce the deficit to one after the 16th, but their effort wasn't enough and Team USA triumphed by one hole.

Meanwhile, further back on the course, the inspired Spanish pairing of young Sergio Garcia and the rather more experienced Jose Maria Olazabal were working wonders in their fourball against David Toms and Ryder Cup rookie Brett Wetterich. Garcia was on his way to a four-point total in the tournament, and he and Olazabal ran out comfortable winners, by 3&2.

But Stewart Cink and debutant JJ Henry were fighting back for the

BELOW America's Tiger Woods (left) and Jim Furyk plot their next move

ABOVE Paul McGinley
(right) shakes hands
with JJ Henry on the
18th green, oblivious to
the streaker diving into
the water

USA. They came back from three down after nine holes to halve their match with Paul Casey of England and the debutant Swede Robert Karlsson.

Their efforts proved of limited value in the end, however. The experienced and successful pairing of that man Clarke and England's Lee Westwood were never behind as they recorded a one-hole victory.

So as the team captains rallied their troops for the Friday afternoon four-somes, the scoreboard showed Europe leading by 2.5 to 1.5. It was the ideal platform for a successful defence of the trophy, and Europe did not look back.

Happy Europeans
watch the action during
the singles matches on
the final day

Every single match that Friday afternoon went to the 18th green, however, and three of the four were halved.

The only winning pairing that afternoon proved to be Luke Donald of England and the ubiquitous Garcia. And their opponents? Woods and

Furyk, victors in their fourball match a few hours before. In deteriorating weather, Furyk fired his approach shot at the 18th into the water and Donald and Garcia were able to seal a 2-up win.

In the first of the other three foursomes, Harrington and fellow Irishman Paul McGinley halved with Chad Campbell and Zach Johnson, despite having been two holes up with three to play, while David Howell of England and Stenson chalked up an identical result in their match with Cink and David Toms.

The other Friday foursome pitted Montgomerie and Lee Westwood against world number two Phil Mickelson and the feisty Chris DiMarco – and it proved just as fascinating in reality as it had looked on paper.

The relief was evident on Monty's face as he holed a six-foot birdie putt to halve the match. Two holes earlier, the big Scot had found water with his approach shot and the Americans had looked all set for a win.

So the European team was able to look back on a satisfying first day from the vantage point of a hard-fought 5-3 lead. More drama was to follow on day two.

Saturday morning's fourballs provided little comfort for the American team, who emerged with 1.5 points to Europe's 2.5. Their sole victory came in a Stenson/Harrington v Scott Verplank/Johnson match, by the margin of 2&1.

The red-hot Garcia and Olazabal

BELOW Jose-Maria Olazabal (left) of Europe shakes hands on the 17th green with Phil Mickelson of USA after winning his singles match

BELOW Stewart Cink (left) is congratulated on winning his final day singles match on the 15th green by Sergio Garcia

took up where they had left off on Friday, recording an emphatic 3&2 win over Mickelson and DiMarco. Westwood and Clarke tore similarly into Woods and Furyk and came up with an identical winning margin.

The other fourball saw Casey and Karlsson sharing the honours with Cink

and Henry. With the tournament score at 7.5 – 4.5 in Europe's favour, the stage was set for an extraordinary afternoon foursomes session.

One moment from that Saturday afternoon will be remembered above all others. It came at the Palmer Course's par-3 14th, where Casey and Howell were comfortably in control against Cink and Johnson. Casey selected a 4-iron from his bag and gazed at the pin 215 yards away. Moments later the match was over as his tee shot disappeared into the cup.

A hole in one is never a bad thing. On this occasion, it gave the European duo a stunning 5&4 victory and some valuable extra time for rest and recuperation.

It almost goes without saying that Garcia continued his winning ways that afternoon. He and Donald played seven holes against Mickelson and Toms before breaking the deadlock when the Americans double bogeyed. They soon went two up before being pegged back to all square –

ABOVE Sergio Garcia accepts the adoration of the K Club crowd

but they were not to be denied. At the end of a thrilling match, Garcia and Donald had notched up a 2&1 win.

Meanwhile, Woods and Furyk were doing their damnedest to make a fight of it, and doing it pretty well. Their 3&2 win over local favourites Harrington and McGinley proved the only USA win of the afternoon, however. In the other match, the Montgomerie/ Westwood pairing halved with Campbell and Taylor.

ABOVE Darren Clarke
(left) celebrates after
making a 110 ft putt

RIGHT Colin
Montgomerie (left)
and Lee Westwood
line up a putt

As the last of the players trooped into the clubhouse, Europe were sitting pretty with a 10-6 lead. They were clearly the favourites to win the trophy outright – for an unprecedented third consecutive time – and needed just four points from the Sunday singles matches to do so. It's a fair bet that not many European players were dwelling on the last time the team had held a similar lead going into the final day. On that occasion, in 1999 at Brookline, the USA

had overhauled them to take a staggering 14.5 - 13.5 victory.

The stalwart Montgomerie launched Europe's singles campaign, and he launched it in style. His superlative bunker shot at the 18th helped him to a 1-up triumph over Toms.

Next up was Garcia, who found he could not replicate his wonderful fourball and foursome play in the face of some marvellous golf from Cink. The man from Alabama sank a 50ft birdie at the 12th hole and closed out a convincing 4&3 win.

Woods was also in determined mood and, recovering from the shock of seeing his caddie drop his 7-iron in a lake, saw off the challenge of Karlsson by 3&2.

Furyk was having no early luck on the K Club's greens, in contrast to opponent Casey, but he came up with an eagle at the 16th to put the pressure on the young Englishman. Casey promptly holed from 20ft at the 17th and clinched a 2&1 win.

It was nip and tuck between Donald

BELOW Ian Woosnam gets the champagne treatment on the clubhouse balcony after Europe's win in the Ryder Cup

and Campbell before that famous Donald putt at the 17th, while McGinley and Henry fought out a halved match. By that time, European golf fans were celebrating anyway.

As the champagne corks popped and bar staff checked their supplies of Guinness, play was continuing and Europe were on their way to that astonishing 18.5 – 9.5 winning margin.

For the record, Verplank (a 4&3 win for the USA over Harrington), Westwood (2-up against DiMarco), Olazabal (2&1 against Mickelson) and Howell (5&4 against Wetterich) were the men wishing they were in the clubhouse with the others.

All over the K Club and a long way further afield, tears were flowing along with the bubbly.

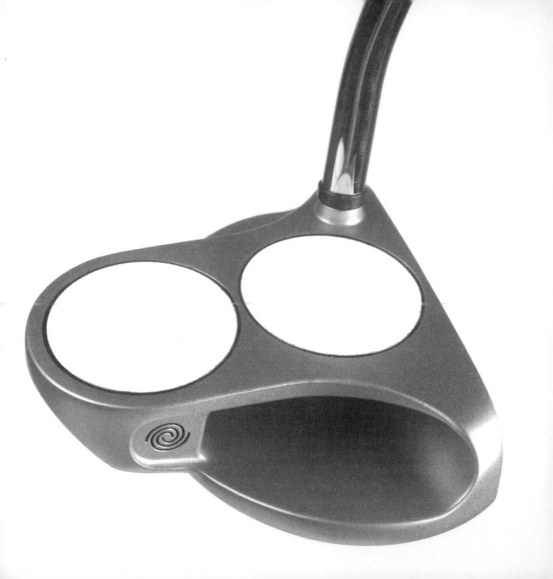

The pictures in this book were provided courtesy of

GETTY IMAGES
www.gettyimages.com

Design and artwork by Jane Stephens

Image research by Ellie Charleston

Published by Green Umbrella Publishing

Series Editors Jules Gammond and Vanessa Gardner

Written by Patrick Morgan and Steve Newell